KT-546-926

LONDON
THE WEEKENDS START HERE

LONDON THE WEEKENDS START HERE

Fifty-two weekends of things to see and do

TOM JONES

Virgin BOOKS

CONTENTS

INTRODUCTION 9

SPRING

The Countryside of Croydon	12
Artistic London	17
Trees of London	21
William Morris's London	24
Easter London	28
American London	31
Betjeman's London	36
Japanese London	39
Churchyard London	43
Treasure Hunters' London	46
French London	49
Poets' London	54
Russian and Eastern European London	58

SUMMER

The Kings of Kingston and Richmond	64
Wild London	68
Wartime London	72
The Back Roads of Bexley and Bromley	76
Along the River Lea	80
Park Life London	85
Beside the Sleepy Thames	90
Tea and Cakes of London	93
Towers of London	97
The Edges of Essex	102
Jubilee Line London	105
Along the Green Chain	109
August Bank Holiday London	112

AUTUMN

Pirates' London	118
The Houses of Hampstead	121
Immigrant London	126
Sporting London	130
Boozy London	133
Revolutionary London	138
Italian London	142
The Gentle Brent	146
Engineers' London	149
Perspectives on London	153
Political London	158
Hidden South Bank and Bankside	161
The Northern Heights	165

WINTER

Nordic London	170
Dickens's London	173
Subterranean London	176
Highlights of Hackney	180
Lions of London	185
Yuletide London	188
Fishermen's London	193
Musical London	197
Scientific London	200
Ancient London	203
Georgian London	206
Circus London	211
Bibliophiles' London	215

INDEX 218

FOR CATHERINE

ACKNOWLEDGEMENTS

With thanks to Nicola Barr and Elen Jones for their support, to David Doran and Sophie Yamamoto for their visual flair and Mary Chamberlain for her eye for detail.

Thanks as ever to Susan, Peter, Stephen and Cynthia Jones for their ongoing help and humour, and new thanks to Catherine Forrester for her unwavering support during all aspects of the research of this book. Thanks also to Jon Searle, Jemima Warren, Alison Griffin, Ronnie Whittington, Tom Knapp and others for joining me on trips out in London.

Finally, thanks to all those who share the best of their own London, including Ian Mansfield, Jane Parker, Matt Brown, Lindsey Clarke, Malcolm Edwards, Laura Porter, Sue Hillman, Diamond Geezer and countless others.

INTRODUCTION

London is the ultimate weekend city, with enough to see and do to fill a lifetime of weekends, no two the same. Greater London covers more than 600 square miles, with thirty-two different boroughs, and the financial City at its beating heart. Within it are people from every country of the world, and the stories and histories of all the earth's inhabitants are laid out ready for discovery.

Though Londoners work some of the longest hours in Europe, at the weekends the city is a playground. Unshackled from their desks, residents have a chance to explore an unrivalled range of cultural, artistic, historical and natural experiences, discovering the unexpected before another Monday morning rolls around.

London is home to over 8 million people, with another 10 million tourists visiting from abroad each year, and countless others making trips from the rest of Great Britain. It is impossible to see more than a fraction of the city in a single weekend, but approaching it weekend by weekend is one of the best ways to experience it.

The most enjoyable weekends you will ever spend in London are those which you discover for yourself, or that occur by happy accident. This book aims to help you join the dots of the finest city in the world, one weekend at a time.

SPRING

Spring is a fine time to be in London, the moment when the capital's parks and gardens come back to life, and a change in the clocks offers longer evenings. Birds return from their winter adventures, bringing spring songs. Blossom and new leaves appear in the trees, whilst baby ducks and cygnets swim in the rivers and lakes, and the city farms greet newborn lambs. The spring is a festive time, with St Patrick's Day, the Chelsea Flower Show, the Boat Race and May Day offering plenty of opportunities to get outdoors. London comes alive in spring, drawing throngs of visitors seeking to enjoy everything it has to offer.

THE COUNTRYSIDE OF CROYDON

Were it not for the forward-thinking Londoners of the inter-war years, the city might have sprawled out unchecked in every direction. Instead of endless rows of housing estates, the Metropolitan Green Belt secures the availability of green space. In Croydon, it protects North Downs landscapes and ensures that there are still grazing animals, country pubs and woodland walks a stone's throw away.

The Countryside of Croydon
CATCH THE TRAM TO SOUTH NORWOOD COUNTRY PARK

Once part of the Great North Wood, since 1989 South Norwood Country Park has been a 125-acre green public space. It features a wild-flower meadow, wetland reserve and lake, and attracts over 100 different species of bird.

From a mound at one end it is possible to see the Docklands skyscrapers and Crystal Palace transmitter, whilst trams drift quietly right through along the Tramlink. There is also a pitch-and-putt golf course and visitors' centre.

www.croydon.gov.uk
Albert Road, SE25 4NF
Harrington Road Tramlink station

The Countryside of Croydon
SEEK SUSTENANCE AT THE WHITE BEAR, FICKLESHOLE

The quaint White Bear at Fickleshole is a beautiful, quintessentially rural sixteenth-century inn, squeezed between two farms in a tiny hamlet inside the M25. Cyclists on National Cycle Route 21 regularly whizz past or stop to sample the extensive menu and fine ales.

A sculpture of a white bear stands outside, the original of which was stolen during Canadian troops' high jinks in the 1940s. The pub is also said to have two resident ghosts.

www.the-whitebear.com
Fairchildes Lane, Warlingham, Surrey CR6 9PH
New Addington Tramlink station

The Countryside of Croydon
WANDER RIDDLESDOWN'S TRACKWAYS

A large area of ancient chalk scrub and grassland owned by the City of London Corporation, Riddlesdown is still grazed by animals. It bears evidence of thousands of years of human activity, with a prehistoric earthwork known as Newe Ditch trackway and a Roman road that probably ran southwards from London towards ironworks and the coast.

The site is also known for its population of yew trees, accessible by paths on the lower slopes; for ancient Coombes Wood; and for the Neolithic stone axes which have been found there.

www.cityoflondon.gov.uk
Riddlesdown Common, Croydon, CR8 1EE
Riddlesdown railway station

ADMIRE THE VIEW FROM ADDINGTON HILLS

Rising to 140 metres (460 feet) above sea level, Addington Hills comprise 130 acres of heathland and woods overlooking Croydon town centre, purchased between 1874 and 1919. They combine with Croham Hurst and Shirley Heath to create a chain of popular open spaces.

As part of the celebration of 1,000 years of Croydon in 1963, a viewing platform was added, with views to Shooters Hill, Epping Forest, Fulham and on clear days even Windsor Castle. Hungry visitors might also enjoy the Royal Garden Chinese Restaurant, operated by the Cheung family.

www.croydon.gov.uk
Addington Hills, Shirley Hills Road, Upper Shirley, CR0 5HQ
Coombe Lane Tramlink station

The Countryside of Croydon
SPOT FOXES IN FOXLEY WOOD

First recorded in the Surrey Assize Rolls of 1279 as Foxle, when it was much bigger, Foxley Wood combines with Sherwood Oak as 26½ acres of mixed woodland and grassland, purchased for the community in 1937 in the Green Belt scheme.

The wood is on a steep chalk hill, with the older, ancient woodland at the top and newer trees below, offering a haven for wildlife, with fresh greenery and woodland flowers making it especially inviting in spring. Walking trails are marked by little wooden signposts.

www.friendsoffoxley.co.uk
Foxley Wood, Kenley, Croydon, CR8 2HT
Kenley railway station

Weekend Tips

Riddlesdown, Foxley Wood, Happy Valley and Farthing Downs can be connected on foot as part of a fine day's walk, with lunch at the Fox Inn at Coulsdon Common (Fox Lane, Coulsdon Common, CR3 5QS).

The Countryside of Croydon
WALK THE HAPPY VALLEY

A peaceful valley consisting of downland chalk, grassland and woodland in the Green Belt on the edge of Old Coulsdon, the Happy Valley is rich with wild flowers, over twenty-five species of butterfly and birds such as skylarks, kestrels, cuckoos, nightingales and woodpeckers.

A short distance across the fields, the ancient and peaceful Grade I listed church of St Peter and St Paul at Chaldon contains a twelfth-century wall painting of heaven and hell.

www.croydon.gov.uk
Happy Valley Park, Old Coulsdon, Croydon, CR5 1DH
Coulsdon South railway station

The Countryside of Croydon
CROSS FARTHING DOWNS

Adjoining the Happy Valley, Farthing Downs and New Hill cover 235 acres of chalk grassland, designated a Site of Special Scientific Interest in 1975 as the 'most extensive area of semi-natural downland habitats remaining in Greater London'.

Though suburban settlements are clearly visible in the valleys beneath, from the top it is easy to imagine standing here as an ancient inhabitant. Evidence of human activity from all periods has been recorded, with Neolithic pottery, an Iron Age pit, Roman artefacts and mid-seventh-century Anglo-Saxon burial mounds.

www.cityoflondon.gov.uk
Farthing Downs, Coulsdon, Croydon, CR5 1DA
Coulsdon South railway station

ARTISTIC LONDON

Whilst court artists such as Holbein, Van Dyck and Rubens came to London in the sixteenth and seventeenth centuries, it was not until the founding of the Royal Academy of Arts in 1768 that the climate was right to foster great British artists. Constable and Turner flourished, and by the dawning of the Victorian period, Britain had become the world's most powerful nation, attracting artists from all other countries. London has remained a leading world city for art, and still competes for supremacy with New York, Rome and Paris.

Artistic London
BUY BRUSHES AT L. CORNELISSEN & SON

Any shop that has supplied not only Turner and Constable but also Tracey Emin and Damien Hirst with art materials must be doing something right, and L. Cornelissen & Son has a rich pedigree.

This art supplies shop has been trading since 1855, when it was established in Covent Garden by a Belgian lithographer who fled Paris following the 1848 revolution.

www.cornelissen.com
105 Great Russell Street, WC1B 3RY
Tottenham Court Road tube station

Artistic London
SEE THE STREET ART OF EAST LONDON

The area around Shoreditch and Brick Lane has been a centre for street art for over a decade. It is a democratic medium and freshly sprayed graffiti jostles with officially sanctioned works like those on the Village Underground's Holywell Lane wall and Ben Eine's shop-shutter alphabet and murals. Work by scene darlings such as Banksy and Stik can also be seen.

The newer ad-hoc works change so often that it can be useful to seek a guide from one of the various walking tours of the area.

www.shoreditchstreetarttours.co.uk
Shoreditch, E1
Liverpool Street tube and railway station

Artistic London
EAT AT THE SOUTH LONDON GALLERY

Since 1891, Camberwell's South London Gallery has been bringing ordinary south Londoners to its much-loved Arts and Crafts-style stone and brick building on Peckham Road to view its fine collection of contemporary art.

A critically acclaimed project, finished in 2010, allowed the gallery to develop new spaces both for its exhibits and for its café and restaurant, Number 67. This is open daily, serving everything from a cup of tea and a biscuit to a full evening menu.

www.southlondongallery.org
65–67 Peckham Road, SE5 8UH
Peckham Rye overground and railway station

Weekend Tips

The number 3 bus runs from Crystal Palace to the Dulwich Picture Gallery, which has a great restaurant, and is a short walk from the excellent Crown and Greyhound pub (73 Dulwich Village, SE21 7BJ).

SEEK PISSARRO'S INSPIRATION IN SOUTH LONDON

French Impressionist Camille Pissaro came to south London in 1870–71, living for a while at 77a Westow Hill, South Norwood, and inevitably seeking inspiration from his surroundings.

Today, his oil paintings of Fox Hill in Upper Norwood and the Avenue in Sydenham hang in the National Gallery, whilst a view of Lordship Lane station, painted from a footbridge in Sydenham Hill Woods, can be found at the Courtauld Institute of Art.

Plaque at 77a Westow Hill, SE19 1TZ
Crystal Palace overground and railway station

VISIT ENGLAND'S OLDEST ART GALLERY

Peacefully set in leafy grounds on the edge of Dulwich Village, Dulwich Picture Gallery grew out of a collection of paintings owned by Dulwich College. It was added to when Sir Francis Bourgeois left the college his own art collection.

Bourgeois stipulated that the public must be allowed to view the works in a specially constructed gallery, for which he left the money. It opened in Sir John Soane's stunning building in 1817, and is now home to one of the greatest collections of old masters in the country.

www.dulwichpicturegallery.org.uk
Gallery Road, SE21 7AD
North Dulwich railway station

BROWSE PICCADILLY ART MARKET

A consciously lowbrow alternative to the multi-million-pound art sales being held in auction houses and private galleries a few streets away, Piccadilly Art Market takes place along the northern edge of Green Park at weekends. Pictures extracted from the backs of vans are displayed on the railings.

In the market's heyday, many paintings were by struggling artists who went on to greater things, as Roy Petley famously did in the 1970s. Though today most are inexpensive and pedestrian prints, it is still fun to browse.

Piccadilly, W1
Green Park tube station

EXPLORE 500 YEARS OF BRITISH ART

Tate Britain's unrivalled national collection explores British art from 1500 to the present day, continuing a service with which it has provided the nation since its opening in 1897 as the National Gallery of British Art.

As British art has changed, so the gallery has adapted to ensure it remains just as relevant. While often hosting the controversial Turner Prize exhibition, it stays true to its history with projects such as the opening of the Clore Gallery in 1987 to house an extensive collection of work by Turner.

www.tate.org.uk
Millbank, SW1P 4RG
Pimlico tube station

TREES OF LONDON

There are an estimated 7 million trees in Greater London, with a fifth of its area under tree canopy, and 8 per cent taken up by woodland. Trees not only help to make London prettier and less unrelentingly urban, they also remove carbon dioxide and pollution from the atmosphere, helping to make Londoners happier and healthier. Some silent guardians have been standing for longer than the modern city has existed.

Trees of London
CAMP OUT IN ABBEY WOOD

Few imagine it is possible to camp out in London, let alone in a woodland setting surrounded by nature, but the Caravan Club's site at Abbey Wood in south-east London is open to all, year round.

Boasting 210 pitches, with fifty set aside for tents, the site has all modern conveniences such as hot showers and Wi-Fi. The crowd is distinctly international – as well as residents of Kent and Sussex, holidaymakers from the Continent take advantage of trains from London Bridge which take less than thirty minutes.

www.caravanclub.co.uk
Abbey Wood Caravan Club Site, Federation Road, SE2 0LS
Abbey Wood railway station

Trees of London
SEEK THE VETERAN TREES OF GREENWICH PARK

There are nearly 4,000 trees in Greenwich Park, and whilst most are under a century old, fifty-two gnarled sweet chestnut trees are much older, planted in 1664 for Charles II.

The park's oldest tree, Queen Elizabeth's Oak, lies in a quiet corner. It was around 600 years old when it died in the nineteenth century, but was held up for another 150 years by ivy before coming down in a storm in 1991. Another highlight is one of the country's biggest shagbark hickories.

www.royalparks.org.uk
Greenwich Park, Greenwich, SE10 9NF
Maze Hill railway station

Trees of London
VISIT THE QUEEN'S ORCHARD

A secret walled garden of fruit trees, edible plants and ponds, the Queen's Orchard is found behind a beautiful metal gate in the north-eastern corner of Greenwich Park. It was first planted in the seventeenth century – official records date its existence to at least 1693.

The orchard fell into disuse in 1976 when the Greenwich Hospital Estate sold it to Greenwich Council, but it has since been replanted with fruit and vegetables, and historic varieties of fruit trees dating back to the 1500s.

www.royalparks.org.uk
Greenwich Park, Greenwich, SE10 8QY
Maze Hill railway station

Trees of London
TAKE THE ICE AGE TREE TRAIL

Found in Geraldine Mary Harmsworth Park, beside the Imperial War Museum, the Ice Age Trees project takes visitors on a journey back in time, with a walk around the thirty-four ancient species of British tree which date from the retreat of the ice after the last Ice Age.

Designed by Trees for Cities, the trail uses only those species which had established themselves before Britain became an island, attempting to raise awareness of native trees.

www.southwark.gov.uk
Geraldine Mary Harmsworth Park, Lambeth Road, SE1 6ER
Lambeth North tube station

GAZE UP AT THE EMBANKMENT PLANES

When the Victoria Embankment was constructed between 1864 and 1870, it was planted with a type of tree known as the London plane, a deciduous hybrid of an Oriental and American plane that grows up to 30 metres (100 feet) tall and is tolerant of pollution.

Today, London planes are ubiquitous in the centre of the city, but those on the Embankment are some of the finest. Trees for Cities cites the example on the corner of Embankment and Horse Guards Avenue as one of the Great Trees of London.

www.treesforcities.org
Embankment, SW1
Westminster tube station

Weekend Tips

The Pavilion Tea House in Greenwich Park (Blackheath Avenue, SE10 8QY) is a pleasant spot, and the Mary Beale Restaurant at West Lodge Park is known for its afternoon teas.

CLIMB TREES IN TRENT COUNTRY PARK

Covering 413 acres of green space in the London Borough of Enfield, Trent Park, once part of the royal hunting forests of Henry IV, opened in 1973. Plenty of woodland remains, with a choice of Moat Wood, Williams Wood and Oak Woods, all surrounding a house that was commandeered during the Second World War, and is now part of Middlesex University.

The park is also home to a treetop adventure park, privately run by Go Ape, featuring swings, high ropes and a zip wire.

www.trentcountrypark.com
Trent Country Park, Cockfosters Road, Enfield, EN4 0PS
Cockfosters tube station

SEE THE BEALE ARBORETUM

Founded in 1963 by Edward Beale, the Beale Arboretum occupies 35 acres within the grounds of the West Lodge Park Hotel, and includes mature trees planted by the park's former owner John Cater in the mid-1800s.

The arboretum features 800 different types of tree from around the world, as well as national collections of hornbeam and swamp cypress, and trees planted by Lord Mayors of London and local MPs.

www.bealeshotels.co.uk
West Lodge Park, Cockfosters Road, Hadley Wood, Hertfordshire, EN4 0PY
Cockfosters tube station

WILLIAM MORRIS'S LONDON

One of the great designers of the Victorian era, and the leader of the Arts and Crafts movement, William Morris was born in March 1834 in Walthamstow, then a reasonably small suburban village. It was the beginning of a lifelong relationship with London which saw him living in Bloomsbury, at Red House in Bexleyheath and at Kelmscott House in Hammersmith while running businesses in Bloomsbury's Red Lion Square, at 449 Oxford Street and in Merton.

EXPLORE THE RED HOUSE GARDEN

When William Morris and Philip Webb designed Red House in Bexleyheath in 1859, they were keen for the gardens to be an extension of the house, divided into sections resembling rooms and 'clothing' the house, integrating it with its surroundings.

Plant names were included in Webb's designs, and the nature of the oasis that they created is evident today. The regularly openeed house and gardens inspired many Morris & Co. designs.

www.nationaltrust.org.uk/red-house
Red House, Red House Lane, Bexleyheath, DA6 8JF
Bexleyheath railway station

GO SHOPPING AT MERTON ABBEY MILLS

By the turn of the seventeenth century, Merton Abbey Mills had become a centre for textile manufacturers with its dye-friendly chalk stream.

In 1881, Morris & Co. moved workshops with Liberty & Co. to an old calico-printing works there, making Merton Abbey Mills the focal point of the Arts and Crafts movement. The site is now a village, with independent shops, a weekend craft market and a riverside pub bearing Morris's name.

www.mertonabbeymills.org.uk
Merton Abbey Mills, SW19 2RD
South Wimbledon tube station

VISIT THE WILLIAM MORRIS GALLERY

The grand house that was home to Morris from 1848 until 1856 has been preserved in his memory for over sixty years. It was constructed around 1750, taking its original name, the Water House, from the homestead moat still behind it in Lloyd Park.

Morris was born at nearby Elm House in 1834, and interactive displays within the gallery allow visitors to explore what the neighbourhood would have been like when he walked its streets. Morris & Co. originals are combined with information about his life and works and temporary exhibitions.

www.wmgallery.org.uk
Lloyd Park, Forest Road, Walthamstow, E17 4PP
Walthamstow Central tube and railway station

WIlliam Morris's London
SEE THE TUDORS' HUNTING LODGE

Built in 1543 by order of Henry VIII, and renovated in 1589 for his daughter, Queen Elizabeth's Hunting Lodge still sits on the edge of Epping Forest, once a popular spot for royal hunting. It has changed little since Tudor times.

William Morris came to the lodge as a child when living in Walthamstow, taking inspiration from the countryside and from the tapestries that hung here. He later recalled his 'first acquaintance with a room hung with faded greenery' and the 'impression of romance' that it gave him.

www.cityoflondon.gov.uk
Rangers Road, Chingford E4 7QH
Chingford railway station

Weekend Tips

There is a good café at Red House (see page 25), and The Anglesea Arms in South Kensington (15 Selwood Terrace, SW7 3QG) and the riverside The Dove in Hammersmith (19 Upper Mall, W6 9TA) are great pubs.

WIlliam Morris's London
STEP INSIDE HOLY TRINITY SLOANE SQUARE

Once described by the Poet Laureate Sir John Betjeman as 'the cathedral of the Arts and Crafts movement', Holy Trinity Sloane Square is a stunning church designed by architect John Dando Sedding and completed in 1890.

Interior decorations were closely supervised by William Morris and Edward Burne-Jones, and their most eye-catching creation is the huge east window, the largest ever manufactured by Morris & Co.

www.holytrinitysloanesquare.co.uk
Sloane Street, SW1X 9BZ
Sloane Square tube station

WIlliam Morris's London
VISIT 7 HAMMERSMITH TERRACE

The former home of Emery Walker, Arts and Crafts pioneer and friend and typeface mentor to Morris, 7 Hammersmith Terrace is described by the Emery Walker Trust, which opens it for pre-booked tours, as 'the last authentic Arts and Crafts interior in Britain'. Nearby Kelmscott House, home of the William Morris Society, is also open some afternoons.

The house has maintained its original interior with wallpapers, hangings, furniture and textiles by Morris & Co., Philip Webb and William De Morgan.

www.emerywalker.org.uk
7 Hammersmith Terrace, W6 9TS
Stamford Brook tube station

William Morris's London
DRINK TEA IN THE V&A'S MORRIS ROOM

The V&A's Refreshment Rooms combined to make the world's first museum restaurant, an important innovation for which the nation's top designers were recruited. Morris designed the western room, originally known as the Green Dining Room, and construction was completed in 1869.

The Morris Room is deep green, decorated with leaves, Elizabethan-style panelling, stained glass and figures painted by Edward Burne-Jones and Philip Webb. Elsewhere in the museum, Morris's work includes numerous wallpaper designs and pieces of furniture.

www.vam.ac.uk
V&A Museum, Cromwell Road, SW7 2RL
South Kensington tube station

EASTER LONDON

Easter is a time of relaxation and celebration in London, when a long weekend often combines with the start of more spring-like weather to raise spirits. Alongside its important religious significance, the pagan aspects of renewal and new life are marked, as London's city farms welcome new births, and plants in parks and gardens begin to bounce back to life.

ATTEND THE WIDOW'S BUNS CEREMONY

Every Good Friday at the Widow's Son pub in Bow, another hot cross bun is added to a net above the bar in a ceremony that remembers the legend of a widow who once lived in a cottage on the site.

On Good Friday 1824, the widow's sailor son set out to sea, asking his mother to bake him some hot cross buns. He never returned, but his mother continued to bake buns every Good Friday, and leave them waiting for him. Today, sailors attend every year for the ceremony.

75 Devons Road, Bow, E3 3PJ
Devons Road DLR station

WITNESS THE BUTTERWORTH DISTRIBUTION CEREMONY

Victorian legal publisher Joshua Whitehead Butterworth founded a charity with £22 and 10 shillings to offer assistance each Easter to local widows, and hot cross buns to children.

The Butterworth Charity allowed a sixpence each for twenty-one of the poorest widows of the parish of Smithfield, the rest to be spent on hot cross buns. Each Good Friday, the parishioners of St Bartholomew the Great still gather for a distribution ceremony.

www.greatstbarts.com
St Bartholomew the Great, West Smithfield, EC1A 9DS
Barbican tube station

MEET EASTER ANIMALS AT SPITALFIELDS CITY FARM

Established by local volunteers embracing the urban good life during the 1970s, Spitalfields City Farm attempts to bring a bit of the country to its small east London farmyard a short distance from Brick Lane.

In springtime, the farm is alive with young animals including chicks and baby rabbits, and has also been known to hold its Oxford vs Cambridge Goat Race over the Easter weekend, which attracts large crowds.

www.spitalfieldscityfarm.org
Spitalfields City Farm, Buxton Street, E1 5AR
Shoreditch High Street overground station

CELEBRATE EASTER AT ST PAUL'S

Though modern Easter is celebrated by the non-religious as a springtime festival of renewal, its Christian importance is still central, with Holy Week remembering the last week of Jesus's life, and Easter Sunday commemorating the resurrection.

At St Paul's Cathedral, as well as special religious services each day, Holy Week and Easter see a seasonal programme of events, with music recitals, art installations, processions and special family activities to recognise the importance of this time of year.

www.stpauls.co.uk
St Paul's Churchyard, EC4M 8AD
St Paul's tube station

BUY ELABORATE EGGS AT PRESTAT

The Queen's chocolate shop, Prestat, was established in 1902 by Antoine Dufour, a Frenchman who invented the chocolate truffle at the end of the nineteenth century. Today, it still trades from a small shop in Princes Arcade on Piccadilly, making it one of London's oldest chocolate shops.

Prestat offers hand-crafted chocolates and truffles all year round, but really comes into its own at Easter, with beautifully packaged eggs made using recipes which date back more than a hundred years.

www.prestat.co.uk
14 Princes Arcade, Piccadilly, SW1Y 6DS
Piccadilly Circus tube station

Weekend Tips

Close to Prestat, Fortnum & Mason is also known for its Easter treats, including eggs made by Audrey's, an East Sussex chocolate shop that makes around 2,000 unique eggs for the store each season.

SEE THE MOND CRUCIFIXION

Painted by Raphael in the early years of the sixteenth century, the Mond Crucifixion has hung in Room 60 at the National Gallery since it was bequeathed in 1924, following the death of German-born industrialist Ludwig Mond.

The painting was once part of the side-chapel altar at the Church of San Domenico at Città di Castello, northern Italy, not far from Raphael's home town of Urbino. It shows Jesus on the cross, with the Virgin Mary and St John the Evangelist on either side.

www.nationalgallery.org.uk
The National Gallery, Trafalgar Square, WC2N 5DN
Charing Cross tube and railway station

SEEK AN EASTER ISLAND MOAI

Though nobody knows much about where they came from, Easter Island is synonymous with the Moai, monolithic statues carved in volcanic basalt from around 1000 AD until the second half of the seventeenth century.

One of the statues, which weighs around four tons, was 'collected' by the crew of HMS *Topaze* when they visited Easter Island in 1868. Named *Hoa Hakananai'a*, or 'stolen friend', it now stands in Room 24 at the British Museum.

www.britishmuseum.org
Room 24, British Museum, Great Russell Street, WC1B 3DG
Tottenham Court Road tube station

AMERICAN LONDON

The thirteen colonies that signed the Declaration
of Independence in 1776 were all part of the British
Empire, and London and America had already been
linked for more than a century by then. The *Mayflower*
set off from Rotherhithe in 1620 carrying the Pilgrim
Fathers, and the first Governor of Virginia, Captain John
Smith, was buried at St Sepulchre-without-Newgate
Church. Founding fathers Benjamin Franklin and John
Adams spent time in London and Presidents John
Quincy Adams and Theodore Roosevelt both chose to
marry here. Since then, thanks partly to the shared effort
in the First and Second World Wars, London has been a
vital port of call for all American politicians and tourists
on their European tour.

American London
EXPLORE BENJAMIN FRANKLIN'S HOME

The only remaining home of Founding Father Benjamin Franklin is located close to Charing Cross station. Here he lodged on and off with widow Margaret Stevenson between 1757 and 1775, when he returned to Philadelphia.

The story of the scientist, philosopher, inventor and diplomat is told through a 'museum as theatre experience' led by an actor playing his landlady's daughter Polly Hewson. It offers an insight into Franklin's London life, including his love of airing himself in the upstairs windows, and his swims in the Thames.

www.benjaminfranklinhouse.org
36 Craven Street, WC2N 5NF
Charing Cross tube and railway station

American London
PAY TRIBUTE TO HONEST ABE

Though Abraham Lincoln, sixteenth President of the United States of America, never came to London, his towering figure remains a powerful presence at the centre of our democracy, with a huge statue standing in front of Middlesex Guildhall, on Parliament Square.

This replica of Augustus Saint-Gaudens's statue *Abraham Lincoln: The Man*, which stands in Lincoln Park, Chicago, was unveiled in July 1920, to celebrate a century of peace between Britain and the USA.

Parliament Square, SW1A 3BD
Westminster tube station

American London
FIND THE SITE OF THE TEXAS LEGATION

Accessed via a doorway marked with a number 3 beside wine merchant Berry Bros. & Rudd, tiny Pickering Place was the diplomatic address of Dr Ashbel Smith and the representatives of the independent Republic of Texas from 1842 until it joined the United States in 1845.

In 1963, the Anglo-Texan Society arrived to install a commemorative plaque, which can still be seen alongside a second installed in 2013. In the 1980s, some Texans also managed to pay off the legation's outstanding debt to the neighbouring wine merchant, its original landlord.

Pickering Place, 3 St James's Street, SW1A 1EG
Green Park tube station

ORDER A 'SECRET BURGER' AT JOE ALLEN

A subterranean slice of North America that has been trading on a Covent Garden back street since 1977, Joe Allen has a sister restaurant in New York, and remains as popular as ever with the pre-theatre crowd.

Joe Allen is known for the worst-kept secret in the London culinary scene. Its unlisted 'secret burger', once prepared for only the most special VIP guests, is now usually available to anyone with the courage to order off-menu.

www.joeallen.co.uk
13 Exeter Street, WC2E 7DT
Covent Garden tube station

Weekend Tips

Christopher's (18 Wellington Street, WC2E 7DD) is Covent Garden's other American restaurant, whilst just along the street from the Whitechapel Bell Foundry (see page 34), Tayyabs (83–89 Fieldgate Street, E1 1JU) serves good Punjabi cuisine.

GO BOWLING AT BLOOMSBURY LANES

The basement of Bloomsbury's Tavistock Hotel boasts eight ten-pin bowling lanes, styled to make visitors feel they have stepped straight into a twee mid-twentieth-century Californian bowling alley.

The Lanes also has a well-stocked bar, some karaoke booths, table football and an occasional DJ, as well as American-style food served by Ray's Pizza and Diner.

www.bloomsburybowling.com
Basement of the Tavistock Hotel, Bedford Way, WC1H 9EU
Russell Square tube station

VISIT THE CHURCH WHERE A PRESIDENT MARRIED

On 2 December 1886, Theodore Roosevelt walked from Brown's Hotel to St George's Hanover Square to marry Edith Carow. The US Embassy is only half a mile away, and many US servicemen worshipped here during the Second World War.

Though Roosevelt was not the first US President to wed in London (John Quincy Adams married at All Hallows-by-the-Tower), the event brought many more American weddings to a church that also witnessed those of George Eliot, Percy Bysshe Shelley and Benjamin Disraeli.

www.stgeorgeshanoversquare.org
St George's Hanover Square, St George Street, W1S 1FX
Oxford Circus tube station

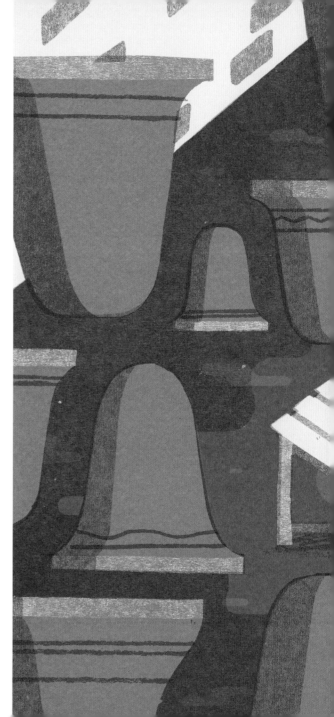

American London
TOUR THE WHITECHAPEL BELL FOUNDRY

Perhaps Britain's oldest manufacturing company, founded in 1570, the Whitechapel Bell Foundry is where the Liberty Bell – hung on the Pennsylvania State House and rung to mark the reading of the Declaration of Independence on 8 July 1776 – was cast.

Though the Liberty Bell was not a great advertisement, as it cracked soon after arrival in Philadelphia, the foundry has a strong pedigree, having cast Big Ben, Christ Church Oxford's Great Tom and bells for St Paul's and Westminster Abbey. Regular tours are available.

www.whitechapelbellfoundry.co.uk
32/34 Whitechapel Road, E1 1DY
Whitechapel tube station

BETJEMAN'S LONDON

A celebrated poet, writer and broadcaster whose tireless campaigning helped to save some of the capital's most important Victorian architectural treasures, Poet Laureate Sir John Betjeman was born in London in 1906. He lived in the city for most of his life, at Highgate, Chelsea and Cloth Fair, celebrating the architecture and places he encountered in poems, articles and radio and TV broadcasts, and helping to protect them for future generations as a founding member of the Victorian Society.

Betjeman's London
STAY AT 43 CLOTH FAIR

Number 43 Cloth Fair, which is within earshot of Smithfield Market, was home to Betjeman from 1954 until 1973, and is now let to holidaymakers by the Landmark Trust, a charity established in 1965 to rescue historic and architecturally interesting buildings.

Betjeman lived and wrote peacefully here, working surrounded by papers and with a secretary taking dictation, before they decided to pack up for the day and pop off to drink champagne at a nearby bar – often Coltman's in Aldersgate Street, long since closed.

www.landmarktrust.org.uk
43 Cloth Fair, Smithfield, EC1 7JQ
Barbican tube station

Betjeman's London
VISIT ST PANCRAS STATION

Betjeman saw the architectural value of stations as public buildings, and it was his foresight and appreciation which helped to save the Victorian buildings of St Pancras – including George Gilbert Scott's Midland Grand Hotel and William Henry Barlow's train shed – from destruction.

When the train shed was completed in 1868, it was the largest single-span roof in the world, and it is easy today to see why Betjeman considered it so important. A statue of him stands on the upper terrace of the station, marvelling at the roof.

www.stpancras.com
St Pancras Station, Euston Road, N1C 4QP
King's Cross St Pancras tube and railway stations

Betjeman's London
DRINK IN THE EUSTON TAP

Though Betjeman won many battles against those who threatened London's Victorian architecture, his biggest loss was the campaign to save the 1837 Euston Arch which once stood proudly above the entrance to Euston station.

Though little evidence of the arch itself remains, two classical lodges can still be found flanking the space, each bearing the names of destinations served by the London & North Western Railways. One houses a tiny beer bar, the Euston Tap, and the other the Cider Tap.

www.eustontap.com
East and West Lodges, 190 Euston Road, NW1 2EF
Euston tube, overground and railway station

Betjeman's London
RIDE THROUGH METROLAND

It is perhaps a little odd that one of Betjeman's best-known works is a BBC TV documentary about a suburban railway line, but the 1973 celebration of life in the areas served by the Metropolitan line seized viewers' imaginations.

The term 'Metro-land' had been coined by the Metropolitan Railway in 1915 for marketing purposes, and was used until the 1930s to promote sales of housing in the suburbs to London's north-west. In the film, Betjeman rode from Baker Street to Amersham, where the line still terminates.

Baker Street station, Marylebone Road, NW1
Baker Street to Amersham tube stations

Betjeman's London
WANDER IN HARROW CHURCHYARD

When Betjeman appeared on BBC Radio 4's *Desert Island Discs* in April 1975, he told Roy Plomley: 'I wasn't at Harrow, but I can somehow think I was there', and his eponymous poem imagines Harrow on the Hill as a rocky island in a turbulent sea.

The poem sees the churchyard of St Mary's full of sailors' graves as rolling waves thunder in Metroland below. The church, originally consecrated in 1094, was remodelled by St Pancras station's Sir Giles Gilbert Scott in the 1840s.

www.betjemanpoetrycompetition.com
St Mary's Church, Church Hill, Harrow on the Hill, HA1 3HL
Harrow on the Hill tube and railway station

Weekend Tips

The Metropolitan line is the only way to travel through Metroland, although some trains are quicker. The Betjeman Arms at St Pancras station does good breakfasts, and the Mahogany Bar at Wilton's is very good.

Betjeman's London
STROLL IN BEDFORD PARK

Described by Betjeman as 'the most significant suburb built in the last century, probably the most significant in the Western world', Bedford Park was laid out in 1877 by Norman Shaw as a self-contained village with a pretty church, St Michael and All Angels, and a pub, the Tabard Inn, both of which are still open.

www.bedfordpark.org
Bedford Park, W4
Turnham Green tube station

Betjeman's London
WATCH A SHOW AT WILTON'S MUSIC HALL

The world's oldest surviving Grand Music Hall, Wilton's had stood on Graces Alley off Cable Street for over a century when it was scheduled for demolition as part of the post-Blitz clearances of the 1960s. Betjeman joined a number of notable voices in campaigning to save it.

The campaign was successful, but the hall remained derelict and under threat until it began to be reopened as a theatre and concert hall in the late 1990s. Thanks to the Wilton's Music Hall Trust, extensive works have been undertaken to protect the building.

www.wiltons.org.uk
1 Graces Alley, E1 8JB
Tower Gateway DLR station

JAPANESE LONDON

Though two Japanese sailors – Christopher and Cosmas – returned with navigator Thomas Cavendish following his circumnavigation of the globe in 1588, London had virtually no Japanese population until the nineteenth century, when the government in Tokyo sent its first mission to Europe. Japanese residents in London still numbered only a few hundred by the turn of the twentieth century, but the Japan–Britain Exhibition held at White City in 1910 did a lot to raise awareness of the country among Londoners, and to cement Anglo–Japanese relations. Today, estimates put the Japanese-born population in London at around 20,000, and regular festivals celebrate the country's culture.

CHILL IN THE HOLLAND PARK KYOTO GARDEN

The Kyoto Garden in Holland Park was created as part of London's 1992 Japan Festival by a team sponsored by the Kyoto Chamber of Commerce. It is a peaceful place, with an ornamental pond filled with koi carp and a waterfall.

The garden, laid out in traditional Japanese style, commemorates the centenary of Britain's friendship with Japan, conveniently forgetting that the formal gardens and woodland which make up Holland Park only came into public ownership after Holland House was bombed in the Second World War.

www.rbkc.gov.uk
Ilchester Place, W8 6LU
High Street Kensington tube station

EXPERIENCE THE KOBE EARTHQUAKE

In the Natural History Museum, right at the top of a huge escalator which passes through a giant model of Earth made from iron, zinc and copper, the Volcanoes and Earthquakes Gallery offers visitors the chance to experience the effects of Japan's 1996 Kobe earthquake.

A recreation of a supermarket interior, the simulator mixes real footage caught on security cameras on the day of the earthquake with equipment that shakes the floor and shelves to demonstrate the destructive power of an 8.9-magnitude earthquake.

www.nhm.ac.uk
Natural History Museum, Cromwell Road, SW7 5BD
South Kensington tube station

SEE THE ART OF THE DAIWA FOUNDATION

The Daiwa Foundation was established in 1988 to encourage closer Anglo–Japanese ties, and as well as arranging exchanges of students between the UK and Japan, it also hosts a range of events each year, including art exhibitions at its Japan House Gallery.

Japan House also hosts courses, meetings and study groups on a variety of subjects, promoting understanding of Japanese art and culture.

www.dajf.org.uk
Daiwa Foundation Japan House, 13/14 Cornwall Terrace (Outer Circle), NW1 4QP
Baker Street tube station

GO SHOPPING AT THE JAPAN CENTRE

A one-stop shop for any Japanophile in London, the Japan Centre first opened in 1980 on Brewer Street selling books and martial arts equipment. Nowadays, its flagship store on Shaftesbury Avenue is London's best shop for all things Japanese, with food, books and homewares, and even its own sushi academy.

The chain also has a cash and carry in Acton and various other smaller enterprises, serving Japanese people working in London, students, visitors and Brits with an interest in Japanese food and culture.

www.japancentre.com
19 Shaftesbury Avenue, W1D 7ED
Piccadilly Circus tube station

EAT AT ZAIBATSU JAPANESE RESTAURANT

Squeezed between Trafalgar Cafe and the budget-friendly Hardy's Free House on Trafalgar Road in Greenwich, Zaibatsu is a popular Japanese fusion restaurant that gets rave reviews for its sushi, sashimi, noodles and tempura.

Often busy, Zaibatsu offers quality food at reasonable prices, with friendly staff and a popular bring-your-own policy.

www.zaibatsufusion.co.uk
96 Trafalgar Road, SE10 9UW
Maze Hill railway station

RELAX IN THE SOAS JAPANESE ROOF GARDEN

The Japanese-inspired roof garden at the University of London's School of Oriental and African Studies was opened as part of the Japan 2001 celebrations, marking the 110th anniversary of the UK's Japan Society.

The garden was designed by Peter Swift as a space for contemplation and meditation, adapting the principles of Japanese garden design to suit the British climate. It has a *karesansui* (dry landscape) with rocks, a chequerboard of lemon thyme and grey pebbles and a water basin engraved with the Kanji characters, promoting forgiveness.

www.soas.ac.uk
Thornhaugh Street, Russell Square, WC1H 0XG
Russell Square tube station

FIND FUDŌ MYŌ-Ō

A highlight of the Japanese collection at the British Museum, Fudō is one of the Myō-ō, 'Kings of Light', a guardian deity of Vajrayana Buddhism. The fierce-looking statue of him engulfed in a huge flame dates from the twelfth century.

Fudō Myō-ō is depicted as he often is in mythology, with wrathful staring eyes and a pair of fangs. As well as a rope, he holds a sword for cutting through the evils of the world of illusion to reveal reality.

www.britishmuseum.org
Rooms 92–94, British Museum, Great Russell Street. WC1B 3DG
Tottenham Court Road tube station

Weekend Tips

If you do make it as far as Zaibatsu, consider a drink afterwards at the Plume of Feathers (19 Park Vista, SE10 9LZ) or the riverside Cutty Sark (4–6 Ballast Quay, Greenwich, SE10 9PD).

CHURCHYARD LONDON

It is not only the tombs and memorials that evoke another age in London's graveyards. Many of the tiny churchyards dotted around the capital date from a time when it was little more than a series of small villages linked to the heaving mass of the City of London by country lanes, where the only traffic was horse-drawn carriages and herds of cattle and sheep being driven to the markets at Smithfields. As such, they often offer echoes of an earlier London, pieces of countryside where birds and plants live peacefully without a care for the urban sprawl that surrounds them.

VISIT THE GARDEN MUSEUM

The church of St Mary-at-Lambeth had already been de-consecrated in 1977 when Rosemary and John Nicholson came looking for the graves of royal gardeners and plant hunters John Tradescant the Elder and Younger. Alarmed to discover that the church was awaiting demolition, they formed the Tradescant Trust.

The church has since been re-roofed and the Museum of Garden History houses gardening-related exhibitions. The highlight is the seventeenth-century knot garden, where the Tradescants' graves lie alongside those of Elias Ashmole, co-founder of Oxford's Ashmolean Museum, and Captain Bligh of the *Bounty*.

www.gardenmuseum.org.uk
The Museum of Garden History, Lambeth Palace Road, SE1 7LB
Lambeth North tube station

ATTEND ST JAMES'S SATURDAY MARKET

The market at St James's Church, Piccadilly, is a relatively new phenomenon, first held in 1981 as part of the Piccadilly Arts Festival, and regularly since 1984.

The market runs six days a week, with arts and crafts on offer on Saturdays until 6 p.m. The neat little rows of stalls are all in the shadow of Christopher Wren's masterpiece of brick with Portland stone, which also houses a coffee shop with al fresco tables.

www.piccadilly-market.co.uk
197 Piccadilly, W1J 9LL
Piccadilly Circus tube station

Weekend Tips

There is also a café at St James's Piccadilly and at the Garden Museum, and plenty of food and drink options in Covent Garden and at St Pancras Station.

Churchyard London

SEE THE MOSAICS IN ST JOHN'S CHURCH YARD

Based in studios in the crypt of St John's Church Waterloo, Southbank Mosaics is a social enterprise responsible for creating more than 250 mosaics across London, with over twenty changing mosaics in the churchyard.

The collection includes four sculptural seats, the largest of which is dedicated to homeless people who have lived and died on the streets. Near St John's, a poignant mosaic on the walls of the Waterloo Action Centre in Baylis Road remembers popular street sweeper Dave Squires.

www.southbankmosaics.com
St John's Crypt, 73 Waterloo Road, SE1 8UD
Waterloo tube and railway station

Churchyard London

SEEK PEACE AT ST PAUL'S COVENT GARDEN

A peaceful oasis in the heart of one of London's busiest districts, the beautiful graveyard at St Paul's Covent Garden, closed to burials since 1853, is now home to flower beds and trees laid out neatly in a compact garden.

Nicknamed the 'actors' church', attracting those from nearby theatres, St Paul's was built by Inigo Jones and completed in 1633. Its churchyard, entered by three passages from Bedford Street, Henrietta Street and King Street, once contained the statue of Charles I now found on Whitehall.

www.actorschurch.org
St Paul's Churchyard, Bedford Street, WC2E 9ED
Covent Garden tube station

TREASURE HUNTERS' LONDON

Still one of the richest cities in the world, London has a history stretching over thousands of years, in which time trade, piracy and war have brought back treasures from around the globe. At its heart, the Tower of London has been home to one of the most important treasure collections of all time since the eleventh century, and two of the largest diamonds ever found, the Cullinan and Koh-i-Noor, can still be seen there. With global billionaires choosing as their home a city which has some of the greatest museum collections in the world, it is hardly surprising that London is filled with treasure.

VISIT THE JEWELLERY QUARTER

Clerkenwell was already known for jewellery by the seventeenth century, but it was not until the 1870s that business began to overflow into Hatton Garden, which by 1885 was home to sixty-seven diamond merchants.

The street was once within the palace of the Bishops of Ely, and was later part of Sir Christopher Hatton's ornate gardens. Though the manufacturing peak when upstairs workshops produced fine jewellery has passed, it still houses hundreds of jewellers.

Hatton Garden, EC1
Farringdon tube and railway station

MARVEL AT THE V&A JEWELLERY GALLERY

The William and Judith Bollinger Gallery at the V&A Museum holds a collection of more than 3,000 pieces tracing the history of European jewellery from Ancient Greece to the present day.

It displays treasures from ancient handmade Celtic jewels to pieces from the great jewellery houses such as Cartier, Boucheron, Chaumet and Fabergé, with watches, tiaras, pendants and other items created for Queen Victoria, Elizabeth I and Tsar Nicholas II.

www.vam.ac.uk
Rooms 91–93, V&A Museum, Cromwell Road, SW7 2RL
South Kensington tube station

SEE THE HOXNE HOARD

The largest hoard of Roman treasure ever discovered in Britain was unearthed by retired gardener Eric Lawes in the Suffolk village of Hoxne in November 1992, as he attempted to find his friend's hammer with a metal detector.

The items are now on permanent display in Room 49 of the British Museum, where their transparent case mirrors the layout of the oak chest in which they were buried.

www.britishmuseum.org
British Museum, Great Russell Street, WC1B 3DG
Tottenham Court Road tube station

WONDER ON THE TREASURE OF SEVEN DIALS

Though Thomas Neale had grand plans when he laid out Seven Dials in the 1690s, with streets radiating out from a central column decorated with six sundials, the area quickly became a notorious slum, described by Dickens as 'lost in the unwholesome vapour which hangs over the house-tops'.

In 1773, rumour spread that treasure was buried beneath the column, and a mob of treasure hunters tore it down. They found nothing. The present column is a faithful replacement, still with six dials despite the extra street which was added to maximise slum dwellings.

Seven Dials, Monmouth Street, WC2H
Tottenham Court Road tube station

Treasure Hunters' London

SEARCH FOR THE LOST CITY OF WATLING STREET

In his book *London Lore*, folklorist Steve Roud recounts legends of a lost Roman city filled with treasure, somewhere along Watling Street north of London. Possibly the ancient settlement of Sulloniacis, it could be found where modern-day Watling Street climbs Brockley Hill, and a sign near the junction with Wood Lane marks the location of a pottery.

Local treasure today takes the form of pockets of countryside. Nearby Stanmore Common and Stanmore Open Space provide pleasant green space, whilst Little Stanmore Common's Caesar's Pond references the Roman garrison who camped locally.

Brockley Hill, HA7
Stanmore tube station

Weekend Tips

Pubs near Chancery Lane include the Seven Stars (53–54 Carey Street, WC2A 2JB) and Ye Olde Cheshire Cheese (Wine Office Court, 145 Fleet Street, EC4A 2BU). Good vegetarian food can be found in Neal's Yard, close to Seven Dials.

Treasure Hunters' London

SEEK THE MISSING GRAFF DIAMONDS

At 4.40 p.m. on 6 August 2009, two men walked into Graff jewellers at 6–8 New Bond Street. When they walked out only a few minutes later, carrying forty-three pieces of jewellery worth around £40 million, they had committed one of the biggest heists in British history.

Though the robbers were caught within a few weeks and received lengthy sentences, none of the jewellery was ever recovered. It is thought it may still be hidden somewhere in the metropolis.

www.graffdiamonds.com
Graff, 6–8 New Bond Street, W1S 3SJ
Green Park tube station

Treasure Hunters' London

ENTER THE LONDON SILVER VAULTS

Opened in 1885 as Chancery Lane Safe Deposit Company, the London Silver Vaults is a collection of underground safes. The 1.2-metre- (4-foot-) thick steel-lined walls even survived a direct hit on the building above during the Second World War.

The Vaults now houses thirty specialist shops boasting one of the world's largest collections of fine antique silver, with prices ranging from £10 to over £100,000.

www.silvervaultslondon.com
Chancery Lane, WC2A 1QS
Chancery Lane tube station

FRENCH LONDON

Though the English Channel provides a natural barrier, London is actually closer to Calais than it is to the borders with Wales and Scotland, so it is hardly surprising that London and France have long retained close ties, and the capital is still home to a large Francophone population. Indeed, at the French elections in 2012, London was France's sixth biggest city in terms of population and elected an 'MP for London' under the Northern Europe constituency. Ties have never been stronger, and as reluctant as both sides probably are to admit it, London's French immigrants have contributed a great deal to the history and culture of the city.

EXPLORE DE GAULLE'S LONDON

On 17 June 1940, following the fall of France to Nazi Germany, General Charles de Gaulle flew to London from where he was to lead the Free French in exile until the summer of 1944, when the D-Day landings and the Liberation of Paris allowed him to return.

A statue of the General stands outside his wartime headquarters at 4 Carlton Gardens, near a memorial plaque remembering his '*À Tous Les Français*' rallying call, which legend has it was written in the French House in Soho.

4 Carlton Gardens, SW1Y 5AB
Charing Cross tube and railway station

DRINK CAFÉ AU LAIT AT MAISON BERTAUX

Founded in 1871 by Parisian communard refugee Monsieur Bertaux, Maison Bertaux on Soho's Greek Street was one of the first French patisseries in London and today is certainly London's oldest.

Originally sharing its small premises with two prostitutes and a tailor who lived upstairs, Maison Bertaux has modestly expanded into three rooms, and subsequent owners Madame Vignaud and Michel and Tania Wade have ensured it retains its historic charm.

www.maisonbertaux.com
28 Greek Street, W1D 5DQ
Leicester Square tube station

Weekend Tips

Those still hungry after Maison Bertaux and Mon Plaisir can pick up French wine and cheese at Berry Bros. & Rudd (3 St James's Street, SW1A 1EG) and Paxton & Whitfield (93 Jermyn Street, SW1Y 6JE).

SEE THE IMPRESSIONISTS AT THE COURTAULD

Some of the greatest French paintings of the nineteenth century hang in the three rooms of the Courtauld Gallery at Somerset House, in a collection started by industrialist and art collector Samuel Courtauld.

Édouard Manet's *A Bar at the Folies-Bergère* and Paul Gauguin's *Nevermore* compete with works by Claude Monet, Edgar Degas and Paul Cézanne for the attention of gallery-goers, who might otherwise be distracted by those of baroque artists Rubens and Van Dyck or the Bloomsbury Group painters.

www.courtauld.ac.uk
Somerset House, Strand, WC2R 0RN
Temple tube station

DINE AT MON PLAISIR

Mon Plaisir, on Covent Garden's Monmouth Street, was established by the Viala brothers in the 1940s, making it one of London's oldest French restaurants. It even hosted an exiled Charles de Gaulle in 1942.

Though there are other restaurants, such as L'Escargot in Greek Street, which claim to be older, Mon Plaisir's good food, charming French decoration (including a bar from a Lyonnais brothel) and family ownership foster a special customer loyalty.

www.monplaisir.co.uk
19–21 Monmouth Street, Covent Garden, WC2H 9DD
Tottenham Court Road tube station

EAT CRÊPES AT THE KENSINGTON CRÊPERIE

The Kensington Crêperie, on Exhibition Road, is right at the heart of South Kensington's Petite France, and has been serving French pancakes from a Grade II listed former dairy since 2001.

The premises are rich with French paraphernalia. Pictures by well-known artists such as Shimon Mizrahy, continental furniture, traditional tiles and outdoor seating give it a particularly Parisian feel.

www.kensingtoncreperie.com
2–6 Exhibition Road, South Kensington, SW7 2HF
South Kensington tube station

WALK HUGUENOT SPITALFIELDS

In the late seventeenth century, as London was rebuilt following the Great Plague and the Great Fire, thousands of Protestant Huguenots, for whom life in France was becoming increasingly difficult, fled to the relative religious freedom of Britain.

A large number settled in Spitalfields, with silk merchants occupying grand Georgian houses in Wilkes Street, Fournier Street and Princelet Street, where their voices rang out across the rooftops. The nearby Brick Lane Mosque was originally built as a Huguenot church, *L'Eglise Neuve*.

Spitalfields, E1
Shoreditch High Street overground station

French London
READ BOOKS AT
LA MÉDIATHÈQUE

The largest French library in the UK is found in a stunning reading room at the Institut Français du Royaume-Uni in South Kensington, part of a complex that also includes a language teaching centre, a cinema and a French bistro.

Known as La Médiathèque, the library is home to a huge collection of French-language material, with over 30,000 books, DVDs and CDs covering all aspects of French culture and society.

www.institut-francais.org.uk/la-mediatheque
17 Queensberry Place, SW7 2DT
South Kensington tube station

POETS' LONDON

London has inspired many poets, from William Blake, John Keats and Lord Byron who were born in the capital, to Dylan Thomas, Percy Bysshe Shelley and Samuel Taylor Coleridge who made it their home. It has inspired countless verses, and celebrates its poets just as they celebrate the city, burying them among kings and queens in Westminster Abbey and erecting statues to them, such as Lord Byron on Park Lane, Sir John Betjeman at St Pancras and Robert Burns on the Embankment.

SEEK INSPIRATION ON WESTMINSTER BRIDGE

In the early morning of 31 July 1802, William Wordsworth and his wife set off from Charing Cross on the Dover Coach for France to visit a friend.

Wordsworth sat on the roof of the coach in brilliant sunshine, with views to the City and St Paul's Cathedral, and to the Thames awash with tiny boats, and wrote his poem *Composed upon Westminster Bridge*, recording 'The beauty of the morning; silent, bare'.

Westminster Bridge, SW1
Westminster tube station

Poets' London
REMEMBER THE GREATS AT POETS' CORNER

Found in the South Transept at Westminster Abbey, Poets' Corner commemorates some of the greatest British writers, playwrights and poets of all time. The tradition began when Geoffrey Chaucer was buried here in 1400, followed over the years by Samuel Johnson, Charles Dickens, Thomas Hardy and Rudyard Kipling.

Their graves are joined by memorials to William Shakespeare, Sir John Betjeman, William Wordsworth, Robert Burns, Jane Austen and the Brontë sisters, a welcome change from kings, queens and aristocrats.

www.westminster-abbey.org
Westminster Abbey, Deans Yard, SW1P 3PA
Westminster tube station

Poets' London
DRINK TEA AT THE POETRY CAFÉ

On a quiet back street in Covent Garden, the Poetry Café doubles as the headquarters of the Poetry Society, a charity founded in 1909 which aims to promote poetry around the world.

As well as serving tea and cake and a light vegetarian lunch, the café hosts poetry readings and other events most evenings, including a weekly poetry open-mic night.

www.poetrysociety.org.uk
22 Betterton Street, WC2H 9BX
Holborn tube station

Poets' London
READ AT THE POETRY LIBRARY

Found on the fifth floor of the Royal Festival Hall, the Saison Poetry Library is the most comprehensive collection of post-1912 poetry in Britain, with more than 200,000 items.

The library was founded in 1953 by the Arts Council, and aims to stock all poetry published in the UK, with two copies of each book and audio title, one for reference and one for loan. There is also an exhibition space with artists' works inspired by the collection.

www.poetrylibrary.org.uk
Level 5, Royal Festival Hall, Southbank Centre, SE1 8XX
Waterloo tube and railway station

Poets' London
VISIT THE POETS' CHURCH

Popularly known as the Poets' Church, St Giles-in-the-Fields has many poetic links. It was the venue for the wedding of Victorian poets Elizabeth Barrett and Robert Browning, for the baptism of John Milton's daughter Mary and for the joint baptism of the children of Byron and Shelley.

Monuments can be seen to metaphysical poet and politician Andrew Marvell, and to George Chapman, who first translated Homer into English. Both are buried in the churchyard.

www.stgilesonline.org
60 St Giles High Street, WC2H 8LG
Tottenham Court Road tube station

Weekend Tips

In Hampstead, it is worth the walk around the heath to search for nightingales at the Spaniards Inn (Spaniards Road, NW3 7JJ), which is one of London's best pubs.

Poets' London
FALL IN LOVE AT THE WHEATSHEAF

It was love at first sight when Dylan Thomas met dancer Caitlin Macnamara one drunken night at the Wheatsheaf in Fitzrovia, after which they booked into a room at the Restaurant de la Tour Eiffel in Percy Street, charging it to Caitlin's sometime lover, the painter Augustus John.

Fitzrovia at the time was the centre of the literary set, and George Orwell, Anthony Burgess and Julian MacLaren-Ross also drank in the Wheatsheaf, along with other bohemians, when the nearby Fitzroy Tavern became too fashionable.

25 Rathbone Place, Fitzrovia, W1T 1JB
Tottenham Court Road tube station

Poets' London
WATCH FOR NIGHTINGALES IN KEATS'S GARDEN

Though the Spaniards Inn in Hampstead claims that the poem was written in their garden, his friend Charles Brown claims that Keats wrote *Ode to a Nightingale* beneath a plum tree in his own garden in Hampstead.

There is a small charge to enter Keats House, now a museum to the memory of the man who occupied it from 1818 to 1820, but the gardens are free. They are overlooked by a 300-year-old mulberry tree which was growing when Keats lived here.

www.cityoflondon.gov.uk
10 Keats Grove, NW3 2RR
Hampstead Heath overground station

RUSSIAN AND EASTERN EUROPEAN LONDON

Trade with Eastern Europe had become common from the thirteenth century via the Hanseatic League across the North Sea to Poland and the Baltic ports. Although some tabloid commentators would have us believe that people from Russia and Eastern Europe have only lived in London for the past few years, in fact significant populations have been evident since at least the 1880s, when Jewish people settled in east London having fled the pogroms and persecution of Tsar Alexander III. During the Second World War, many members of the free Polish Air Force arrived, some staying after the war had ended, and ties with Eastern Europe have remained strong ever since.

SEARCH FOR THE KGB AT THE BROMPTON ORATORY

During the Cold War, London was a prime location for KGB agents seeking to steal Western secrets. In an age before electronic messaging, the KGB developed a network of Dead Letter Drops in anonymous locations, where messages could be deposited by one agent to be secretly collected later by another agent or representative from the Soviet Embassy.

One such site was at the Brompton Oratory. Messages, microfilm and other small packages were left in the little space behind a column to the left of a small altar inside the entrance. It is said that this spot was used as recently as 1985.

www.bromptonoratory.com
Brompton Road, SW7 2RP
South Kensington tube station

EAT AT THE POLISH HEARTH CLUB

Within the elegant surroundings of the Ognisko Polskie Club, founded in 1940 as a rallying point for the wartime free Polish community in London, Ognisko Restaurant serves Polish and other Eastern and Central European cuisine to appreciative diners.

Whilst the rest of the premises is usually only for members, the Ognisko Polskie Club, or Polish Hearth Club, also hosts a series of regular events including theatrical productions, film screenings and musical recitals, many open to the public.

www.ogniskorestaurant.co.uk
55 Prince's Gate, Exhibition Road, SW7 2PN
South Kensington tube station

ATTEND AN EVENT AT PUSHKIN HOUSE

Officially known as the Russian Cultural Centre, Pushkin House has been a bastion of Russian Culture in London since 1954, hosting events and exhibitions to showcase Russian arts.

In 2005, the Pushkin House Trust bought 5a Bloomsbury Square, which has now become its home, hosting regular film screenings, concerts, lectures and talks, as well as exhibitions of Russian art and a library of Russian literature.

www.pushkinhouse.org
5a Bloomsbury Square, WC1A 2TA
Holborn tube station

Weekend Tips

For those with appetites or wallets unsuitable for Ognisko and the Gay Hussar, there is a good café at the National Gallery, and Ognisko has a bar which serves a lighter menu.

• •

Russian and Eastern European London

HONOUR POLISH PILOTS AT ST CLEMENT DANES

Many Polish pilots, who had escaped as their home country was invaded, fought in the Battle of Britain. The four squadrons who took part are remembered in a Polish Air Force memorial in the floor of St Clement Danes on the Strand, with the Polish White Eagle at its heart.

Another war memorial is found beside the A40 near RAF Northolt, Hillingdon, where No. 303 Polish Fighter Squadron was based, an important reminder of the more than 19,000 Poles who served in the Polish Air Force in Great Britain.

www.raf.mod.uk
St Clement Danes, Strand, WC2R 1DH
Temple tube station

• •

Russian and Eastern European London

ADMIRE BORIS ANREP'S NATIONAL GALLERY MOSAICS

One of the greatest artworks at the National Gallery is found not hanging on a wall but beneath the feet of those who enter via the portico, in the form of four mosaics created by Russian-born artist Boris Anrep between 1928 and 1952.

Alongside 'The Labours of Life' and 'The Pleasures of Life', 'The Awakening of the Muses' on the half-landing features Clive Bell as Bacchus, Diana Mitford as Polyhymnia and Virginia Woolf as Clio, whilst 'The Modern Virtues' depicts Winston Churchill as Defiance fighting a swastika-shaped beast, T. S. Eliot as Leisure and Bertrand Russell as Lucidity.

www.nationalgallery.org.uk
Trafalgar Square, WC2N 5DN
Charing Cross tube and railway station

Russian and Eastern European London
EAT AT THE GAY HUSSAR

The Gay Hussar was established in 1953 by
Cumbrian Victor Sassie, after he spent the
1930s in Budapest as an apprentice to famous
Hungarian restaurateur Karoly Gundel.

A popular lunchtime favourite with Labour
politicians, journalists and artists, whose signed
pictures line the walls, it has been serving
Hungarian food and wine to the people of Soho
for more than fifty years. The pre-theatre menu
is a particular draw in the early evenings.

www.gayhussar.co.uk
2 Greek Street, Soho, W1D 4NB
Tottenham Court Road tube station

Russian and Eastern European London
FIND PETER THE GREAT IN DEPTFORD

Peter the Great of Russia came to Deptford in
1698 to study shipbuilding, staying at Sayes Court,
a house he rented from the diarist John Evelyn,
while he worked incognito in the yards and held
drunken parties.

A rather odd statue stands overlooking the
Thames at the entrance to Deptford Creek, designed
by Mikhail Shemyakin and featuring Peter, a grand
chair and a small, funny-looking man, said to be a
reference to Peter's interest in genetic curiosities.

In front of Greenfell Mansions off Glaisher Street, SE8 3EX
Cutty Sark for Maritime Greenwich DLR station

SUMMER

Summer is an easy season to enjoy, and Londoners do so as well as anywhere else in the world. A long season of walks by the Thames, picnics, ice-cream cones and lying in the park soaking up the sun is usually on offer. If the weather fails to deliver, Londoners are resilient, finding joy in cultural festivals, and cafés and restaurants filled with summer produce, preparing to seize the opportunity for a barbecue as soon as the sun shows its face again. Long evenings allow residents and visitors to make the most of late visits to the park, and enjoy al-fresco festivals, film screenings and arts in reward for a hard day's work.

THE KINGS OF KINGSTON AND RICHMOND

Kingston upon Thames and Richmond have been associated with the Royal Family for more than 1,000 years, and though the Queen's residence has retreated to Windsor, Hampton Court remains a royal palace and there are many places in the boroughs with royal associations.

Here, where once only kings, queens and aristocrats could gain access, ordinary Londoners can now wander in carefully maintained parks and gardens, backing onto the sleepy Thames which once transported the monarch downriver for business at Westminster.

SAMPLE THE ORIGINAL MAIDS OF HONOUR CAKE

Named after the cake that Henry VIII is said to have observed Anne Boleyn and her maids of honour eating at Richmond Palace, the Original Maids of Honour shop was established in 1850 by Robert Newens. It is still run by the same family, having moved to its current premises in 1860.

The bakery prides itself on making everything in-house, and alongside the Maids of Honour, a range of sweet and savoury tarts, cakes, pies, breads and pastries can be eaten in or taken away, often warm from the oven.

www.theoriginalmaidsofhonour.co.uk
288 Kew Road, Kew Gardens, Kew, Richmond, TW9 3DU
Kew Gardens tube and overground station

VISIT KEW PALACE

The smallest of London's royal palaces, Kew Palace is often overlooked, found as it is within the sumptuous surroundings of the Royal Botanic Gardens, but the four-storey seventeenth-century red-brick house originally built by Dutch Merchant Samuel Fortrey is charming.

It was purchased by George III in 1781 as an annex to the White House, to accommodate his expanding family with Queen Charlotte, and remained a royal residence until her death in 1818. It was here that the King was sent to keep him out of public view during the bouts of 'madness' for which he is remembered.

www.hrp.org.uk
Royal Botanic Gardens, Kew, Richmond, TW9 3AB
Kew Gardens tube and overground station

SEE THE SAXON KINGS' STONE

Seven Saxon kings were crowned at Kingston upon Thames during the tenth century. This shift from Winchester was probably as a result of efforts by the House of Wessex to unify England in the face of threats from the Danes, who had controlled territory in eastern England.

Though many dispute its provenance, local tradition dictates that the sarsen stone outside the Guildhall was the stone on which Edward the Elder and six other kings were crowned. It was recovered from the Saxon chapel of St Mary in 1730.

Guildhall Complex, High Street, Kingston upon Thames, KT1 1EU
Kingston railway station

ADMIRE THE VIEW FROM KING HENRY'S MOUND

Traditionally remembered as the place where Henry VIII stood to watch a rocket fired from the Tower marking the execution of Anne Boleyn, today King Henry's Mound is one of a handful of London's protected views, with any development that might block the view towards St Paul's Cathedral strictly prohibited.

In fact the mound significantly pre-dates the Tudor period, and is thought to have originally been a Bronze Age burial mound, used by early Londoners to remember their dead.

www.royalparks.org.uk
Richmond Park, Richmond, TW10 5HX
Richmond tube, overground and railway station

WALK THE RIVER LONGFORD IN BUSHY PARK

A man-made river commissioned by Charles I in the 1630s to bring fresh water to the Royal Parks beside Hampton Court Palace, the Longford flows from the River Colne at Longford, Heathrow, to Bushy Park through more than ten miles of what is now residential west London.

Red and fallow deer use it for drinking and bathing, and it feeds Charles Montagu's Upper Lodge Water Gardens and the Diana Fountain in Bushy Park, as well as the Long Water at Hampton Court and its Jubilee Fountain.

www.royalparks.org.uk
Bushy Park, Teddington, TW11 0EQ
Hampton Wick railway station

Weekend Tips

There are good cafés at Pembroke Lodge in Richmond Park (off Queen's Road, Richmond Park) and Hampton Court Palace, including the Tiltyard, the Privy Kitchen and the Wilderness Kiosk, all within the palace grounds.

The Kings of Kingston and Richmond

STAND ON THE OTHER MERIDIAN

It wasn't until 1884 that Greenwich Royal Observatory was adopted as the world's Prime Meridian. For many years the King's Observatory, Kew, was the home of London's official time.

A metal post beside Thames Path at Kew shows the position of this early meridian line, still marked by obelisks in the Old Deer Park which were used in time calculations. It is even said that the word OK was born at the King's Observatory as the best chronometers, stamped with the Observatory Kew stamp, were 'OK'.

Thames Path between Kew and Richmond, TW9
Richmond tube, overground and railway station

The Kings of Kingston and Richmond

EAT GRAPES FROM THE WORLD'S OLDEST VINE

Planted in 1769, and now more than 36 metres (118 feet) long, the Great Vine at Hampton Court Palace is the world's oldest and largest recorded vine. Originally housed in a glasshouse designed for Queen Mary's tropical plants, it is now covered by its own Vine House, built in 1969.

The vine was originally grown from a cutting taken at Valentines Mansion in Ilford, and still produces between 500 and 700 bunches of grapes, harvested and sold via the palace shops.

www.hrp.org.uk
Hampton Court Palace, East Molesey, KT8 9AU
Hampton Court railway station

WILD LONDON

Some might incorrectly consider London an urban wasteland which supports no natural life, but in fact it is the greenest city of its size in the world, with green spaces covering almost 40 per cent of the city, and roughly 35,000 acres of parks, woodlands and gardens. London's rivers, lakes and wetlands are visited by migratory birds from around the world, whilst mammals such as bats, foxes, rabbits, mice and voles live in the parks and gardens. London's wilder side is at its best in summer, with a great deal to offer the urban explorer, and hundreds of places to find it.

Wild London
GO FORAGING IN LESNES ABBEY WOODS

The ancient Lesnes Abbey Woods are rich with wildlife and home to such a diverse range of plants that they make an excellent ground for the urban forager, with plenty of fungi and woodland plants.

The woods cover more than 200 acres of hillside and in summer they are rich with edible plants, allowing foragers to follow in the footsteps of monks, peasants and Neolithic men in seeking sustenance in the woods.

www.visitlesnes.co.uk
Lesnes Abbey Woods, Abbey Road, Belvedere, DA17 5DL
Abbey Wood railway station

Wild London
HIKE A SECTION OF THE CAPITAL RING

Covering more than 70 miles around London, the Capital Ring links some of the greener, wildlife-rich spaces on the outskirts, taking walkers to wild places such as Wimbledon Common and Richmond Park to the south-west, and Fryent Country Park, Welsh Harp Reservoir and Highgate Woods to the north.

The full distance is divided into fifteen linear walks. Distinctive green signs mark the route so that no one gets lost, and London's excellent transport network means that walkers can easily return home to their own beds at the end of a long day.

www.walklondon.org.uk

Wild London
SEEK LONDON'S PEREGRINE FALCONS

London provides a surprisingly healthy habitat for scores of different species of birds, some of the rarest and most unexpected of which are the peregrine falcons – the RSPB lists over twenty pairs.

Misty and Houdini are known to nest in the City, and have been seen on the roof of Tate Modern, where the RSPB have encouraged tourists to view them through telescopes. Other nests have been seen at Marlowe House in Sidcup, on the roof of Charing Cross Hospital and at the House of Commons.

www.london-peregrine-partnership.org.uk

Wild London
EXPLORE BROCKLEY AND LADYWELL CEMETERIES

Brockley and Ladywell Cemeteries have long been celebrated for dark overgrown corners. Opened in 1858, the combined cemeteries cover 37 acres, a perfect summertime mix of death and nature.

Aside from patches of brambles and gravestone-absorbing undergrowth, the cemeteries are rich with wildlife, including sycamore, horse chestnut, hybrid black poplar and lime trees, and plenty of squirrels. Those wanting some interesting history might seek out the graves of Cuban anarchist writer Fernando Tarrida del Mármol and cycling pioneer George Lacy Hillier.

www.foblc.org.uk
Brockley Grove, SE3
Crofton Park railway station

Wild London
SEE THE WILDER SIDE OF HYDE PARK

Whilst most consider Hyde Park the domain of manicured lawns and immaculate flower beds, it was once part of a wild hunting forest, inhabited by wolves and wild boar.

The wooded glade between the Old Police House and the Royal Parks Nursery still evokes the park's history with huge shady trees, whilst to the north wild-flower meadows have recently been allowed to bloom. Black swans, buzzards and Egyptian geese are known to visit, and eagle-eyed spotters may see bats on the Dell Bridge at dusk.

www.royalparks.org.uk
Hyde Park, W2 2UH
Hyde Park Corner tube station

Weekend Tips

The Cutty Sark (4–6 Ballast
Quay, Greenwich, SE10 9PD)
and Trafalgar Tavern (Park
Row, Greenwich, SE10 9NW)
in Greenwich both serve
good pub food.

Wild London
WALK THE DOLLIS VALLEY GREENWALK

A ten-mile walking route between Mill Hill and
Hampstead Heath, the Dollis Valley Greenwalk
can be broken for a shorter stroll.

The route follows Dollis Brook from Moat Mount
Open Space to Totteridge Fields, before turning
southward towards Hendon and crossing Windsor
Open Space. It briefly follows Mutton Brook as
Dollis Brook merges with it to become the River
Brent, before continuing across two more patches
of ancient woodland, Little Wood and Big Wood,
and finishing at Hampstead Heath.

www.barnet.gov.uk
Dollis Brook, Barnet, EN5
High Barnet to Woodside Park tube stations

Wild London
WATCH THE DEER IN GREENWICH PARK

Though most visitors to Greenwich Park probably
never realise it, a herd of red and fallow deer lives in
quiet isolation at the northern end, as their
predecessors have done ever since the park was first
enclosed in 1427.

They would originally have been allowed to
wander throughout but are now confined to a secret
area known as the Wilderness, beyond the flower
garden. Visitors wishing to see them must negotiate a
winding path, but will usually be rewarded with a
decent sighting.

www.royalparks.org.uk
Greenwich Park, Greenwich, SE10 8QY
Maze Hill railway station

WARTIME LONDON

Between the start of the Blitz on 7 September 1940 and the turning of German attentions to the Eastern Front in May 1941, London was in the front line of the Second World War, and the city remained under threat until the eventual celebration of VE Day on 8 May 1945. Life was hard, with food rationed, whole neighbourhoods destroyed and many areas evacuated altogether. However, Londoners maintained a brave spirit throughout the war, and welcomed many Allied soldiers, either exiled or posted from overseas, with open arms. Echoes of the war can still be seen in London, an event that shaped the city as much as any other.

VISIT THE BATTLE OF BRITAIN BUNKER

When the underground bunker at RAF Uxbridge first became operational on 25 August 1939, ten days before the start of the war, nobody knew what was in store for the brave pilots who were to be directed from the Fighter Command No. 11 Group Operations Room within.

Over the next six years the bunker played a central role in British history, with aircraft guided from here protecting the evacuation of Dunkirk, fighting the Luftwaffe during the Battle of Britain and helping to ensure the success of the D-Day landings.

www.raf.mod.uk
St Andrew's Road, Uxbridge, UB10 0RN
Uxbridge tube station

Weekend Tips

Save time by seeing the pillboxes of Hornchurch Country Park as part of your 'Edges of Essex' weekend instead (see page 102).

REMEMBER THE FALLEN OF RAF BOMBER COMMAND

Unveiled in June 2012 to remember the 55,573 aircrew of RAF Bomber Command from all over the world who lost their lives during the Second World War is a memorial of white Portland stone in Green Park.

At its heart stand seven 2.7-metre-(9-foot-)high bronze airmen, dressed as though they have just returned from a mission, with some looking out towards the horizon, perhaps sadly searching for those comrades who would never return.

www.rafbf.org
Green Park, SW1
Hyde Park Corner tube station

EXPLORE THE IMPERIAL WAR MUSEUM

In the dark days of February 1917, with the First World War at a stalemate, the first shots of the Russian Revolution yet to be fired and the USA still to commit, Liberal MP Sir Alfred Mond wrote to David Lloyd George to propose a National War Museum.

The Imperial War Museum has become one of the world's greatest collections on human conflict, with 10 million items across five branches. The original museum moved to the old Bethlem Royal Hospital in 1936, refurbished in 2014.

www.iwm.org.uk
Lambeth Road, SE1 6HZ
Lambeth North tube station

Wartime London

DESCEND INTO THE CHURCHILL WAR ROOMS

Accessed through a small doorway beneath the Treasury building, the Cabinet War Rooms are where Winston Churchill and his cabinet spent much of the Second World War, protected from the bombs of the Blitz by a layer of concrete up to 3 metres (10 feet) thick.

The rooms also provided occasional sleeping quarters for Churchill and his family and private staff.

Visitors can read about the life of Churchill, and see a special telephone, disguised as a lavatory, for speaking directly to US President Roosevelt.

www.iwm.org.uk
Clive Steps, King Charles Street, SW1A 2AQ
Westminster tube station

Wartime London

STAY IN A HOTEL ROOM WHERE WAR WAS DECLARED

On 8 December 1941, the Dutch government in exile declared war on Japan from Room 36 at Brown's Hotel in Mayfair. Queen Wilhelmina and members of her government had escaped from the Netherlands before the surrender in 1940, and the room was home to Prime Minister Pieter Gerbrandy for five years.

Future US President Theodore Roosevelt also slept the night before his wedding in the hotel in 1886. Other guests include Napoleon III of France and Haile Selassie I of Ethiopia, and it provided refuge for Elisabeth, Queen of Belgium, and George II of Greece.

www.roccofortehotels.com
33 Albemarle Street, W1S 4BP
Green Park tube station

Wartime London

MOURN THE CHURCH THAT WENT TO AMERICA

Where until the 1960s the blitzed shell of Christopher Wren's Church of St Mary Aldermanbury stood behind the Guildhall, now little but a few memorials and a modest public garden remain. The church is nearly 4,000 miles away in the grounds of Westminster College in Fulton, Missouri.

The college gymnasium was famously the venue for Winston Churchill's 1946 'Iron Curtain' speech, and following the decision to create a National Churchill Museum at Fulton, permission was given for the church's 7,000 stones to be transported at a cost of $2 million, and reassembled there.

www.cityoflondon.gov.uk
St Mary Aldermanbury Garden, Aldermanbury, EC2 7HP
St Paul's tube station

Wartime London

EXPLORE THE PILLBOXES OF HORNCHURCH PARK

Though RAF Hornchurch was extensively landscaped in the 1970s and 1980s to create Hornchurch Country Park, some of the original defences can still be seen, with pillboxes, bunkers and Tett turrets slowly being swallowed up by grass and weeds.

The park through which the River Ingrebourne flows is a wildlife haven. Birds and insects thrive in its river, lakes, grassland, reedbeds, woodland and hedges, blissfully unaware that this place repelled Zeppelin attacks in the First World War and launched Spitfires in the Second.

www.ingrebournevalleyfriends.org
Airfield Way, Hornchurch, RM12
Elm Park tube station

THE BACK ROADS OF BEXLEY AND BROMLEY

Many residents of Bexley and Bromley do not consider themselves Londoners at all. They live in Kent, regardless of where an arbitrary local authority might place them, and they are happy living in Kent. Since 1965, both have been part of Greater London, but there is a different feeling out here, with more space and even woodland and fields and villages thanks to the Green Belt, yet still within easy reach of central London.

GET AFLOAT
IN DANSON PARK

Found within the grounds of Danson House, a Palladian villa designed by Bank of England architect Sir Robert Taylor, Danson Park's 12-acre lake is now home to a water-sports centre.

The centre is approved by the Royal Yachting Association, and offers sailing, windsurfing and canoeing tuition, as well as traditional rowing-boat hire.

www.bexley.gov.uk
The Boathouse, Danson Road, Welling, DA6 8HL
Welling railway station

The Back Roads of Bexley and Bromley
VISIT HALL PLACE AND GARDENS

An impressive Tudor mansion set in more than 60 acres of gardens, Hall Place was built for former Lord Mayor of London Sir John Champneys in 1537, and is today in the care of the Bexley Heritage Trust.

Though the house is interesting, the gardens are the real highlight of any visit, featuring topiary shaped like the Queen's Beasts heraldic symbols, a sub-tropical glasshouse brimming with exotic plants, fish and terrapins, a 'Butterfly Jungles' butterfly house and a grass maze.

www.bexleyheritagetrust.org.uk
Bourne Road, Bexley, DA5 1PQ
Bexley railway station

The Back Roads of Bexley and Bromley
WANDER IN FOOTS CRAY MEADOWS

The River Cray winds its way through 9 miles from Orpington to Crayford Marshes, where it meets the River Darent. It is particularly picturesque at Foots Cray Meadows, where green fields roll down towards a waterway fringed by ancient woodlands.

The Meadows are most beautiful as the river passes under Five Arches Bridge, built in 1781 to a design by Capability Brown, and on the western edge where the fourteenth-century All Saints Church, Foots Cray, is noted for its Norman font.

www.footscraymeadows.org
North Cray Road, Sidcup, DA14 5AG
Albany Park railway station

The Back Roads of Bexley and Bromley
WALK THE FAESTEN DIC TRAIL

Deep within the 300 ancient acres of Joyden's Wood on the Bexley–Kent border, Faesten Dic is an ancient Saxon defensive ditch, constructed around the fifth and sixth centuries as a result of local tribal conflicts.

The woods are now under the management of the Woodland Trust and a waymarked trail follows a circular route along the dyke, beginning and ending on Summerhouse Drive in Joyden's Wood.

www.woodlandtrust.org.uk
Joyden's Wood, Stable Lane, off Vicarage Road, Near Bexley, DA5 2AW
Bexley railway station

The Back Roads of Bexley and Bromley
SEE THE ROMAN VILLA AT ORPINGTON

Orpington would have been little more than rolling countryside between AD 140 and 400, when legions of Roman soldiers passed regularly on their way between Londinium and Roma.

The remains of Crofton Roman Villa were discovered by railway workmen in 1926, saved from destruction in the 1980s and now preserved in a shed beside Orpington Station, cared for by local volunteers. The villa can be visited in summer.

www.bromley.gov.uk
Crofton Roman Villa, Crofton Road, Orpington, BR6 8AF
Orpington railway station

TAKE CHARLES DARWIN'S THINKING WALK

Charles Darwin lived in Down House from 1842 until his death in 1882, and it was in the study here that he wrote *On the Origin of Species*, while conducting experiments in the greenhouse and garden. Both house and gardens are cared for by English Heritage and open to the public.

Darwin rented a neighbouring stretch of land, where he planted a wood and laid down 'The Sandwalk', a gravel path on which he would walk several circuits daily, looking at the view and thinking, right until the final weeks of his life.

www.english-heritage.org.uk
Down House, Luxted Road, Downe, BR6 7JT
Orpington railway station

RELAX IN HIGH ELMS COUNTRY PARK

A 250-acre area of woodland, meadows and parkland, High Elms Country Park was once part of the High Elms Estate, owned by the aristocratic Lubbock family.

Acquired by Kent County Council in 1938 to become a nurses' training centre, the area was adopted as part of the London Borough of Bromley in 1965, and the estate came too. It is now a public park, and its chalk meadows and woodlands are open to the public all year round.

www.bromley.gov.uk
Shire Lane, Orpington, BR6 7JH
Orpington railway station

Weekend Tips

For food and drink, try the riverside café at Hall Place and Gardens, the tea room at Danson House in Danson Park or the George & Dragon (26 High Street, Downe, BR6 7UT), a short walk from Down House.

ALONG THE RIVER LEA

Whilst many of the rivers that once cut through London were re-routed or exiled underground as the great city expanded, the River Lea (or Lee) proved both too useful and too troublesome to be erased from the map. As early as the ninth century, the Danes navigated it to the north, culminating in the Battle of the River Lea, and by the sixteenth century locks were built so that it could be used to bring grain to London. As the city grew, it required water, and many reservoirs fed from the Lea can still be found along the river's route. When its lower marshes proved impossible to develop for housing or industry, they became leisure spaces for residents detached from the countryside.

ADMIRE THE ART OF TRINITY BUOY WHARF

Owned by lighthouse providers Trinity House until 1988, today Trinity Buoy Wharf is home to artists and creative businesses, the prop-making department of the English National Opera and the Drawing School has just been renamed the Royal Drawing School. Thames Clippers run boats on the river and there is an American-style diner.

Public arts here include a Sculpture Park with works by Andrew Baldwin, a small shed commemorating Michael Faraday and Marcus Vergette's Time and Tide Bell, which rings out as high tide arrives.

www.trinitybuoywharf.com
64 Orchard Place, E14 0JY
East India DLR station

TAKE A TOUR OF THE MILLER'S HOUSE

There has been a tidal mill close to the mouth of the River Lea for 900 years, as recorded in Domesday Book. By the thirteenth century, it had become part of the nearby Abbey of St Mary's, Stratford Langthorne, and after the Dissolution of the Monasteries it passed through a number of private owners.

Despite the destruction of the original Miller's House in the Blitz, the main building, which dates back to 1776, remained relatively intact and is open to visitors on Sunday afternoons. It is the world's largest remaining tidal mill.

www.housemill.org.uk
Three Mill Lane, Bromley-by-Bow, E3 3DU
Bromley-by-Bow tube station

WALK THE OLYMPIC PARK

Though the gold medals of Super Saturday are a distant memory, there is still something special about a walk around the grassland and waterways of the Queen Elizabeth Olympic Park, taking in many venues of the 2012 Olympic Games, including the Olympic Stadium, the Copper Box and the London Aquatics Centre.

At 560 acres, it is as large as Hyde Park, and boasts 40 miles of waterways and 111 acres of woods, hedgerows and natural habitats for wildlife.

www.queenelizabetholympicpark.co.uk
Stratford, E20
Stratford tube, DLR, overground and railway station

Weekend Tips

Fatboys Diner and the Bow Creek Café offer sustenance at Trinity Buoy Wharf, whilst there is a friendly café at the House Mill.

CYCLE IN THE LEE VALLEY VELOPARK

The 2012 Olympic Games were sold on their legacy, and have left the people of east London with access to sporting venues they could otherwise only have dreamed of.

In what was once a forgotten corner of the river valley, amateur cyclists can take to professional tracks, taking laps of the Olympic velodrome, making use of a road circuit, testing mountain bike skills on a short section or trying the jumps of the Olympic BMX track.

www.visitleevalley.org.uk
Abercrombie Road, Queen Elizabeth Olympic Park, E20 3AB
Stratford tube, DLR, overground and railway station

Along the River Lea
PLAY FOOTBALL ON HACKNEY MARSHES

Hackney Marshes is the spiritual home of Sunday League Football in London, with more than fifty marked football pitches providing a venue for scores of amateur football matches each week.

The Marshes are grassland drained from the flood plain of the River Lea during medieval times and used for dumping rubble from buildings destroyed during the Blitz. Since 1946, they have been the venue for the matches of the Hackney & Leyton Football League, witnessing the skills of such football greats as Bobby Moore and David Beckham.

www.hackneyandleytonfootballleague.co.uk
Homerton High Road, E9 5PF
Hackney Wick overground station

Along the River Lea
WANDER IN WICK WOODLAND

Wick Woodland is at the southern end of Hackney Marshes. The first trees were planted in 1896, with a row of plane trees along the canal and some native black poplars on Homerton Road.

Between 1996 and 2000, saved from the threat of development, the area formerly known as Wick Field was planted with fresh saplings. Today, alongside the established planes, poplars and ash trees, this woodland wildlife haven boasts field maples, silver birch, rowan, hawthorn, willow, apple and oak trees.

www.hackney.gov.uk/parks.htm
Homerton Road, London, E9
Hackney Wick overground station

Along the River Lea
EXPLORE GUNPOWDER PARK

Under lock and key for over a century as a testing ground for munitions developed at the nearby Royal Gunpowder Mills, Gunpowder Park in Waltham Abbey was opened to the public in 2004 as a country park.

Thanks to the relative lack of human interference, Sewardstone Marsh, Rammey Marsh and Osier Marsh Woodland are rich with wildlife, including water voles, Daubenton's bats, damselflies, woodpeckers and sparrowhawks. There is also a display of butterflies.

www.visitleevalley.org.uk
Sewardstone Marsh, Waltham Abbey, Essex, EN9 3GP
Enfield Lock railway station

PARK LIFE LONDON

Whilst London is a city for every season, the summer reveals all the parks have to offer, with thousands of acres of lush green landscapes and plenty of opportunities to take advantage when the sun decides to show its face. Londoners do take holidays at the beach or abroad, but unlike Paris and other European capitals, the city remains thriving during the summer season. Parks become the city's beating heart, with long evenings and more predictable weather prompting months of parkland festivals and cultural events for visitors and locals.

Park Life London
TAKE A BOAT ON HOLLOW PONDS

Situated beside Whipps Cross Road, the waters of Hollow Ponds are in one of the southern outposts of Epping Forest.

The ponds were dug as a set of gravel pits, and a bathing pool was added as part of an unemployment project in the early years of the twentieth century, fed by natural springs and eventually developed into Whipps Cross Lido. Although this was closed in 1982, boats can be hired from a small jetty.

www.facebook.com/hollow.lake
Whipps Cross Road, E11
Snaresbrook tube station

Park Life London
MEET THE SHEEP AT MUDCHUTE CITY FARM

Mudchute Park and Farm is one of London's largest city farms. In summer, the animals are seen out in the fields and farmyards every day, with sheep, goats and chickens happily enjoying hilltop sunshine, and llamas a short distance away.

Mudchute was originally a dumping ground for spoil and silt from the excavation of Millwall Dock, saved from development in the 1970s. The farm seeks to educate city dwellers about what the animals we eat look like.

www.mudchute.org
Pier Street, Isle of Dogs, E14 3HP
Mudchute DLR station

Park Life London
SIT AMONG THE ROSES IN GREENWICH PARK

In the shadow of red-brick Georgian Ranger's House, home to the Wernher Collection of more than 700 works of art, is Greenwich Park's beautiful semicircular rose garden.

The garden includes over 100 varieties of roses, separated from the rest of the park by a low hedge with alcoves for a number of benches which act as sun traps on bright days. Despite being near the cricket pitch and tennis courts, it maintains a peaceful serenity.

www.royalparks.org.uk
Within Greenwich Park close to Chesterfield Walk, Blackheath, SE10
Maze Hill railway station

Park Life London
GO FOR A WALK IN RUSKIN PARK

Named after writer, artist and local resident John Ruskin, and designed in the early 1900s by London County Council's Chief Officer of Parks, Lt Col. J. J. Sexby, Ruskin Park is a leafy oasis on the borders between Camberwell, Brixton and Herne Hill.

There is a small bandstand hosting frequent summer concerts, some pretty little flower gardens and a pergola, ornamental and wildlife ponds, a kiosk café, and a children's play area and paddling pool.

www.lambeth.gov.uk
Denmark Hill, SE5 8RS
Denmark Hill overground and railway station

RELAX IN BONNINGTON SQUARE GARDENS

A communal garden in one of the more pleasant corners of Vauxhall, Bonnington Square Gardens bills itself as a modern-day pleasure garden. It emerged from the 1970s squatters' housing collective which seized the attractive local railway-workers' cottages, remains of a terrace bombed in the Blitz, saving them from demolition.

Today the Bonnington Square Gardens Association maintains lush sub-tropical plants, trees, a large iron waterwheel and a 'Helping Hand' sculpture. Regular communal working parties ensure things are kept in order.

www.bonningtonsquaregarden.org.uk
Bonnington Square, SW8
Vauxhall tube and railway station

WATCH THE TROOPING THE COLOUR PROCESSIONS

The Queen's official birthday is marked each June by Trooping the Colour on Horse Guards Parade. She inspects her troops amid a great deal of pomp and ceremony, before leading them down the Mall to Buckingham Palace and finally appearing on the palace balcony.

While those who wish to watch from the stands must apply well in advance, spectators are free to line the route along the Mall or the edge of St James's Park, and the event usually features a fly-past by RAF aircraft. Tickets are also available for two rehearsals, the Major General's Review and the Colonel's Review.

www.royal.gov.uk
Horse Guards Parade, Whitehall, SW1A 2AX
Westminster tube station

Weekend Tips

The Bonnington Café, off Bonnington Square, is a celebrated vegetarian café which began life serving food to those visiting a 1980s squat, and now offers hearty meals cooked up by a changing programme of chefs.

Park Life London
SWIM IN THE SERPENTINE LIDO

At the heart of Hyde Park, the Serpentine has been attracting swimmers for over a century. Races began in the 1830s and the Serpentine Swimming Club has held its Christmas Day Race since 1864. A 1930s lido building is open to all those willing to brace the water's often-chilly temperatures, on weekends throughout May and seven days a week from June until early September.

The lido also offers a sunbathing area, a paddling pool and playground for children, and the Lido Café Bar with lakeside tables.

www.serpentinelido.com
The Serpentine Lido, Hyde Park, W2 2UH
Hyde Park Corner tube station

BESIDE THE SLEEPY THAMES

As the Thames weaves its way west through Twickenham and Richmond, it is no longer the raging tidal beast that is seen in the centre of town, but is fringed with parkland, river-meadow islands and weeping willows, with rowing and sailing boats taking advantage of its quieter stretches. After Teddington Lock, the Thames loops sleepily around Hampton Court, before meandering off towards rural Berkshire. The communities along these stretches readily embrace the river, both in the names of their settlements, which are always 'on-Thames', and in their use of its waters for pleasure-boating and riverside attractions.

EXPLORE HAM HOUSE

Designed by Robert Smythson and built in 1610 by naval captain Sir Thomas Vavasour, Ham House was the residence of a number of royals and aristocrats before Charles I's childhood whipping boy, William Murray moved in.

Today, scores visit daily to enjoy the Orangery café and tour the National Trust-run house and gardens, which include a kitchen garden and 'Wilderness' with summerhouses.

www.nationaltrust.org.uk
Ham Street, Ham, Richmond, Surrey. TW10 7RS
Richmond tube, overground and railway station

ADMIRE THE NAKED LADIES

Though York House in Twickenham has passed through the hands of various well-connected courtiers, politicians and aristocrats, it is perhaps best known as the home of Indian industrialist Sir Ratan Tata.

Tata installed many of the garden's elaborate flourishes, including the sunken lawn and the Oceanides statues, known locally as the Naked Ladies, which stand on a rockery and water feature. Carved in Rome by Oscar Spalmach, they came to York House after their original owner James Whitaker Wright committed suicide in the courtroom after being found guilty of fraud.

www.yorkhousesociety.org.uk
Richmond Road, Twickenham, TW1 3AA
Twickenham railway station

DISCOVER THE TWICKENHAM MUSEUM

A fine example of London's fascinating little neighbourhood museums, the Twickenham Museum examines the history of the area over thousands of years, charting famous locals from writers and poets to sailors and soldiers.

www.twickenham-museum.org.uk
25 the Embankment, Twickenham, TW1 3DU
Twickenham railway station

VISIT THE ORLEANS HOUSE GALLERY

Based in what remains of Orleans House, built in the eighteenth century for Secretary of State for Scotland James Johnston, and once home to exiled future King Louis Philippe II of France, the Orleans House Gallery is Richmond upon Thames's municipal art gallery.

The house was once home to Mrs Nellie Ionides, an avid collector who left the property and her art to the borough in 1962. Though much of the house had been demolished in 1926, the gallery occupies a wing off the grand Octagon and the nineteenth-century stable block to the rear.

www.richmond.gov.uk
Riverside, Twickenham, TW1 3DJ
Twickenham railway station

Beside the Sleepy Thames
WATCH MUSIC AND DRAMA AT GARRICK'S TEMPLE

Constructed by the great eighteenth-century actor, playwright and theatrical manager David Garrick in 1756 as a memorial to the genius of William Shakespeare, Garrick's Temple to Shakespeare is an octagonal domed folly at Hampton, inspired by the Pantheon in Rome.

The Temple gardens are open to the public daily, and a small exhibition on Garrick and Shakespeare is open on summer Sunday afternoons. In the summer there are also occasional Saturday afternoon concerts and plays, and regular evening events.

www.garrickstemple.org.uk
Hampton Court Road, Hampton, TW12 2EA
Hampton Court railway station

Weekend Tips

Those looking for cheaper boat hire can find it at Richmond Bridge Boathouses (Bridge Boathouses, Richmond upon Thames, TW9 1TH), where rowing boats for up to seven people are available to hire.

Beside the Sleepy Thames
SPEND AN AFTERNOON ON THE THAMES

From their boatyard on the lush green Chertsey Meads meadow, the Shields family hire a number of self-drive day boats for those wanting to take to the water and explore the Thames at their own speed.

The largest, *Molly May*, carries twelve people and even has a kettle for those wishing to enjoy a cuppa en route, whilst the smaller *Sea Catch* can be hired for fishing trips, in an area rich with pike and perch.

www.boatgear.info
Chertsey Meads Marine Boatyard, Mead Lane, the Meads, Chertsey, KT16 8LN
Addlestone railway station

Beside the Sleepy Thames
GO WILD SWIMMING IN FERRIS MEADOW LAKE

Though swimming in the Thames is actively discouraged, Ferris Meadow Lake in Shepperton is an exception. Shepperton Open Water Swim uses the beautiful lake as a venue for wild swimming.

Popular with triathaletes and long-distance swimmers, the lake is open throughout the summer as long as conditions are right. When a chill hits, swimmers head down the road to Hampton heated open-air pool, which offers al-fresco swimming 365 days a year.

www.sheppertonopenwaterswim.co.uk
Ferry Lane, Shepperton, TW17 9LH
Shepperton railway station

TEA AND CAKES
OF LONDON

Samuel Pepys's diary records him drinking tea for the
first time in September 1660, and its sale in England is
popularly credited to merchant Thomas Garway, who
started stocking it in the 1650s. Tea, coffee and cake
really began to make their presence felt in London
towards the end of the seventeenth century, with coffee
houses popping up to sell hot drinks around the city as
increased trade and slavery brought sugar prices down.
A once-rare and precious commodity became central
to the British diet, giving birth to the culture of tea
and cake.

Tea and Cakes of London

LEARN THE HISTORY OF TEA AT THE V&A

The V&A Museum offers a range of tours of its extensive collection, focusing on different aspects of history, and the History of Tea tour takes participants on a journey from its origins in China to the tea sets of Victorian Britain.

With quantities of related paraphernalia, including caddies, urns, teapots, cups, bowls and other ceramics, and professional guides who know their subject matter, the tour explains not just the history of tea drinking but also its place in society, technology and international trade.

www.vam.ac.uk
V&A Museum, Cromwell Road, SW7 2RL
South Kensington tube station

Tea and Cakes of London

EXPERIENCE THE WAY OF TEA AT THE BRITISH MUSEUM

The Japanese Galleries at the British Museum feature a reconstruction of a traditional tea house, to which members of the Urasenke Foundation London Branch come regularly to teach Londoners about Chado, the Way of Tea, usually on Friday evenings.

Dressed in traditional clothing, members seek to educate those who may not be aware of this noble art, a Japanese tradition inspired by Zen Buddhism, which has existed for over 400 years.

www.urasenke.co.uk
Room 92, British Museum, Great Russell Street, WC1B 3DG
Tottenham Court Road tube station

Tea and Cakes of London

FIND THE TEA BUSH AT CHELSEA PHYSIC GARDEN

Founded in 1673 by the Worshipful Society of Apothecaries as a place for its apprentices to study plants for use in medicine, the Chelsea Physic Garden takes advantage of a warm urban location to nurture around 5,000 species of plant in neat little beds.

The much-loved Tangerine Dream Café serves delicious tea and cakes either inside or in the garden itself. Visitors can see a tea plant, or *Camellia sinensis*, as well as coffee beans, which grow in the garden's nearby Tropical Corridor.

www.chelseaphysicgarden.co.uk
66 Royal Hospital Road, Chelsea, SW3 4HS
Sloane Square tube station

EAT CAKES FROM KONDITOR & COOK

Since his first shop opened on one of the most attractive street corners in south London in June 1993, in the renovated Queen of Hearts Bakery near Waterloo station, Gerhard Jenne's Konditor & Cook has won praise across the city for its cakes.

Today, the business boasts six locations around London, still under the direction of the German-born pastry chef and celebrated for everything from brownies and cupcakes to bread and bespoke 'cakes by consultation'.

www.konditorandcook.com
22 Cornwall Road, SE1 8TW
Waterloo tube and railway station

TAKE AFTERNOON TEA AT THE FAN MUSEUM

Although you might have to take out a second mortgage to have tea at a central London hotel, the Fan Museum in Greenwich offers a much cheaper option with tea, scones and cake for under £10 and just as much atmosphere.

Tea is served in the romantic but unpretentious Orangery, looking out through French windows onto the small garden. The museum itself is also well worth a look, even for those who think they have no interest in the history of fans.

www.thefanmuseum.org.uk
12 Crooms Hill, Greenwich, SE10 8ER
Greenwich DLR and railway station

BUY TEAS AT THE TEA HOUSE

Established by Christina Smith in 1982, Covent Garden's Tea House caters for Londoners in search of rare and unusual varieties of tea.

As well as more than seventy different types of caffeinated and decaffeinated teas and herbal infusions, the modestly sized shop sells cups, mugs, pots, tea infusers, tea cosies, bowls, tins and boxes sourced from around the world, making it the perfect gift destination for keen tea drinkers.

www.theteahouseltd.com
15 Neal Street, Covent Garden, WC2H 9PU
Covent Garden tube station

Weekend Tips

Thames Clippers services (www.thamesclippers.com) connect the London Eye, a short walk from Konditor & Cook, to Greenwich every twenty minutes and are great fun.

Tea and Cakes of London

TOUR THE *CUTTY SARK*

Part of a wave of new sleek ships originally designed to bring tea to Britain from the East, the *Cutty Sark* was launched on the Clyde in 1869. Serving for more than fifty years, she set speed records on wool transports to Australia.

Following use as a training ship, she came to dry dock in Greenwich in 1954. Having recovered from heavy fire damage in 2007, she is once again open to the public as part of the National Maritime Museum.

www.rmg.co.uk/cuttysark
King William Walk, Greenwich, SE10 9HT
Cutty Sark for Maritime Greenwich DLR station

TOWERS OF LONDON

The Tower of London, founded after the Norman Conquest in 1066, is one of the country's most important buildings. It has played a central role in English history ever since – as a royal palace; a prison which held William Wallace, Anne Boleyn and Guy Fawkes; the birthplace of the Ordnance Survey; and the home of the Royal Armouries. Nearby, Tower Bridge and the Shard combine with it to form a triangle of towers, providing a whistle-stop tour through the city's history.

Towers of London

VISIT BRITAIN'S OLDEST MUSEUM

The Line of Kings, a display of the arms and armour of England's kings and queens within the White Tower at the Tower of London, is the world's longest-running visitor attraction. It was opened in 1660 as a public-relations exercise for the newly restored monarchy.

The White Tower itself was key. Built in 1078 for William the Conqueror, and the oldest remaining part of the Tower of London, it underlined the longevity of the institution of monarchy. The modern displays remain a vital part of any trip to the Tower.

www.royalarmouries.org
Royal Armouries, The Tower of London, EC3N 4AB
Tower Hill tube station

Towers of London

TAKE A TOUR WITH A YEOMAN WARDER

The 'Beefeaters', or Yeoman Warders, are part of the Royal Bodyguard. They have been resident at the Tower of London since at least 1509, and more than thirty still live there with their families.

Modern Beefeaters are former members of the armed forces with a record of at least twenty-two years' service. They give colourful tours of the Tower regularly throughout each opening day.

www.hrp.org.uk
The Tower of London, EC3N 4AB
Tower Hill tube station

Towers of London

SEE THE ROYAL BEASTS EXHIBITION

A menagerie of animals lived at the Tower of London for over 600 years from the early 1200s, with early residents including a polar bear given by the King of Norway in 1251 and an elephant given by Louis IX of France in 1255.

An exhibition in the Brick Tower remembers the menagerie, which by 1704 included six lions, two leopards, three eagles, two owls and a jackal. The Tower remained the animals' home until 1832, when the Duke of Wellington moved them to the newly opened London Zoo.

www.hrp.org.uk
The Brick Tower, The Tower of London, EC3N 4AB
Tower Hill tube station

Towers of London

WATCH THE CEREMONY OF THE KEYS

For more than 700 years, the Ceremony of the Keys has marked the end of the day at the Tower of London.

A few minutes before 10 p.m., the Chief Yeoman Warder locks the gates under the supervision and protection of a military escort. As he returns, he is challenged at the Bloody Tower, leading to an exchange identifying the keys as those of the sovereign before they are taken to the Queen's House. This has become a popular tourist spectacle, and tickets must be applied for well in advance.

www.hrp.org.uk
The Tower of London, EC3N 4AB
Tower Hill tube station

Weekend Tips

Combination tickets are often available online to visit the Tower of London, Tower Bridge and the Shard for a reduced price.

Towers of London

CROSS TOWER BRIDGE

Impressive for being nowhere near as old as it looks, Tower Bridge was designed by City architect Sir Horace Jones in 1884 and opened after his death in 1894.

The bridge's high walks, originally designed so pedestrians could cross the river when the huge hydraulic bascules were raised to allow ships through, now house an exhibition on its construction and operation. From here there are fine views across the whole of London.

www.towerbridge.org.uk
Tower Bridge Exhibition, Tower Bridge Road, SE1 2UP
Tower Hill tube station

Towers of London

ADMIRE THE VIEW FROM THE SHARD

Completed in March 2012, the eighty-seven-storey Shard tower above London Bridge station is visible across Greater London. Visitors can gain access by lift to an indoor viewing gallery on Level 69, and another partially outdoor gallery on Level 72.

The platforms offer some of the best views of London from its highest publicly accessible place, with visibility on clear days of up to 40 miles.

www.theviewfromtheshard.com
32 London Bridge Street, SE1 9SG
London Bridge tube station

ENTER THE BLOODY TOWER

Constructed during the reign of Henry III as a way into the Tower of London from the Thames, the Bloody Tower is reputedly the place where the two 'Princes in the Tower' were murdered in 1483, having been usurped and imprisoned by their uncle, Richard III. Legend has it that they still haunt the Tower today.

It was also where Sir Walter Raleigh was imprisoned for thirteen years for being part of a plot against James I. Other inmates have included Archbishop Thomas Cranmer and the poet Sir Thomas Overbury.

www.hrp.org.uk
The Bloody Tower, The Tower of London, EC3N 4AB
Tower Hill tube station

THE EDGES OF ESSEX

Until the arrival of the railways, places like Upminster and Rainham were country villages at least a day's walk from London, and though they have changed a lot over the past two centuries, thankfully their rural charm has not completely been erased. Out here, despite some patches of unrelenting suburbia, the protection of the Metropolitan Green Belt means that farmers still farm, the birds still sing and streams and rivers still meander towards the Thames. Communities on the edges of Essex do their best to celebrate their connections to rural England with museums and country parks.

MEET THE ANIMALS AT FOXBURROWS FARM

Located within the popular Hainault Forest country park, Foxburrows rare-breeds farm and miniature zoo is home to a number of animals, from geese and donkeys to meerkats, all housed within special enclosures that recreate their natural habitats.

Popular with families, the farm has play areas for all ages, and attracts regular visits from those keen to see animal friends such as Bella the Shetland pony and donkeys Herbie and Zephy.

www.hainaultforest.co.uk
Hainault Forest Country Park, Fox Burrow Road, Chigwell, IG7 4QN
Hainault tube station

WALK BESIDE FAIRLOP WATERS

A former gravel pit which has become a picturesque lake within 300 acres of open countryside, Fairlop Waters has a sailing club, golf course and nature trail.

The lake boasts two islands, and as well as being a popular spot for keen anglers, it has an orienteering course and a new boulder park, offering budding climbers a chance to test their skills over nine specially designed climbing boulders, with varying levels of difficulty. There is also a bar and Greek restaurant.

www.redbridge.gov.uk
Forest Road, Barkingside, IG6 3HN
Fairlop tube station

VISIT UPMINSTER WINDMILL

Upminster Windmill was constructed on top of a hill in 1803 by local farmer James Nokes. Originally wind-powered, it had a steam engine installed and continued grinding flour for more than a century.

When it ceased to be used in 1934 it became derelict, and its future looked uncertain until in 1967 it was repaired and opened to the public. With a new tail fin and sails, the mill is now in the care of the Friends of Upminster Windmill, who hold regular weekend open days.

www.upminsterwindmill.co.uk
The Mill Field, St Mary's Lane. Upminster, RM14 2QL
Upminster Bridge tube station

STEP INTO UPMINSTER TITHE BARN

Home to an interesting collection of agricultural and domestic items, fifteenth-century Upminster Tithe Barn sits at the end of a rough lane, flanked by playing fields and Upminster Golf Course. The local area was once the grounds of Upminster Hall, originally the manor of Waltham Abbey.

The barn is remarkable for its huge beams of English oak, its distinctive weatherboarding and thatched roof. It contains the Upminster Tithe Barn Museum of Nostalgia, covering local history and farming.

www.upminstertithebarn.co.uk
Hall Lane, Upminster, RM14 2TX
Upminster tube and railway station

The Edges of Essex
CYCLE THE INGREBOURNE VALLEY

Opened in May 2013 as cycling charity Sustrans' Route 136, the Ingrebourne Way allows cyclists from Havering and beyond to pedal from the Thames at Rainham to the Essex village of Noak Hill, following the valley of the River Ingrebourne.

There are plenty of opportunities to observe local flora and fauna, with more than sixty species of bird known to breed in the area, one of the largest and most naturally diverse marshlands in Greater London.

www.sustrans.org.uk
Ingrebourne Valley, Hornchurch, RM12 6PB
Upminster tube and railway station

The Edges of Essex
ADMIRE THE VIEW FROM INGREBOURNE HILL

Ingrebourne Hill beside the River Ingrebourne was once a farm, gravel pit and landfill site. It covers more than 130 acres of the London Borough of Havering.

The hill is maintained by the Forestry Commission as a country park with miles of walking and cycling trails overlooking Lake Stillwell, and a community woodland. It offers fine views south towards the Thames and the South Downs, and west towards central London.

www.forestry.gov.uk
Rainham Road, Rainham, RM13 8ST
Rainham railway station

The Edges of Essex
LEARN THE HISTORY OF THE MILITARY THAMES

Beside the Thames near Rainham Marshes, the Purfleet Heritage and Military Centre is housed inside a listed gunpowder magazine, built in 1759 to supply the army and navy during the Napoleonic wars, and used until 1962 for storage by the Ministry of Defence.

The museum explores the history of the area and its relationship with the military history of the nation. Engaging local volunteers are delighted to provide more detail on each display, covering anything from Purfleet during the Blitz to Count Dracula's fictional home.

www.purfleet-heritage.com
River Court, Centurion Way, Purfleet, RM19 1ZY
Purfleet railway station

Weekend Tips

A bicycle is the best way to travel in this part of the world, but the 247 bus and the Upminster-to-Romford train can also be combined with leg power to connect these places.

JUBILEE LINE LONDON

Opened in 1979, and not completed until the dying days of 1999, the Jubilee line is still officially London's newest underground line, despite taking over track which had been part of the Bakerloo line until the 1930s. It covers more than 22 miles between Stratford and Stanmore, and carries over 200 million passengers a year. Though many of them are commuters, the line also connects a range of London's most interesting sights and landscapes, from the hills of north London to the South Bank, the towers of Docklands and the industrial landscapes of east London, all in under an hour.

Jubilee Line London
EXPLORE THE FORMAL GARDENS OF CANONS PARK

Once part of the grand estate of the 1st Duke of Chandos, Canons Park is now maintained by Harrow Council. It is made up of landscape gardens from the eighteenth, nineteenth and twentieth centuries, and is recognised by the Register of Historic Parks and Gardens of Special Interest in England.

A beautiful spot offering a quiet haven in any season, the park is surrounded by listed buildings, including the remnants of the original Canons Mansion, the Temple and St Lawrence Church.

www.friendsofcanonspark.org.uk
Whitchurch Lane, HA8 6QT
Canons Park tube station

Jubilee Line London
VISIT THE STABLES GALLERY AND ART CENTRE

Operated by Brent Council in the beautiful surroundings of Victorian Gladstone Park, the Stables Gallery building was built around 1825 as the stables for Dollis Hill House, former rural retreat of the aristocratic Finch family.

In 1977 the gallery opened as a non-commercial exhibition space for the Brent area, and today it hosts up to twelve exhibitions a year, some paintings of which are hung in the stalls where horses once slept.

www.brentarts.org.uk
Gladstone Park, Dollis Hill Lane, NW2 6HT
Neasden tube station

Jubilee Line London
DRINK IN THE SWISS COTTAGE

Taking its name from an earlier pub built around 1804, a slightly incongruous Swiss Cottage sits on a traffic island beside Swiss Cottage tube station, operated by Sam Smith's brewery, and purpose built in the 1960s.

It is an interesting place, with a mixture of rooms and even an outside seating area where drinkers can relax to the roaring sound of traffic on the A41, imagining they are on an alpine hillside.

98 Finchley Road, London NW3 5EL
Swiss Cottage tube station

MEET THE PELICANS IN ST JAMES'S PARK

Pelicans were first introduced to St James's Park in 1664 as a gift from the Russian Ambassador to Charles II. They were described by diarist John Evelyn, contemporary of Samuel Pepys, as 'a fowle between a stork and a swan'.

Five pelicans still live in the park, at the easterly end of the lake near Duck Island. They are so much a part of Westminster Village that they have even been the subject of debate in the House of Lords. They are fed daily at 2.30 p.m.

www.royalparks.org.uk
St James's Park, Horse Guards Road, SW1A 2BJ
Westminster tube station

Jubilee Line London
EAT AT MASTERS SUPER FISH

Popular with locals and black cab drivers, who come from miles around to dine here, Masters Super Fish is an excellent fish-and-chip restaurant serving ample portions of fish, bought daily from Billingsgate Fish Market.

Available to eat in or take away, the meals come with optional prawns, tea and bread and butter. As good as any chippie in London, Masters Super Fish does a busy trade come rain or shine.

191 Waterloo Road, SE1 8UX
Waterloo tube and railway station

Jubilee Line London
GET BACK TO NATURE AT BOW CREEK ECOLOGY PARK

Near the former site of the Thames Ironworks and Shipbuilding Company is Bow Creek Ecology Park, redeveloped into an urban nature reserve with streams, ponds, footpaths, observation points and seats.

The park, on a peninsula at a bend in the River Lea, is home to a range of flowers and insects during the summer months, when ponds teem with newts and water scorpions. At low tide in season, the mud at Leamouth also attracts flocks of waders such as redshank.

www.visitleevalley.org.uk
Bidder Street, E16 9ST
Canning Town tube and DLR station

Jubilee Line London
WATCH A SHOW AT STRATFORD EAST

In an area which has undergone many changes over the years, the Theatre Royal Stratford East is a constant, tracing its history back to 1884, when actor-manager Charles Dillon engaged architect James George Buckle to convert a wheelwright's workshop into a permanent playhouse.

The theatre offers world-class productions in a listed building, retaining much of the Victorian charm which has helped it to woo audiences for over a century.

www.stratfordeast.com
Gerry Raffles Square, E15 1BN
Stratford tube, DLR, overground and railway station

Weekend Tips

Peyton & Byrne's Inn the Park (St James's Park, SW1A 2BJ) in St James's Park is very good, and there are cafés in Canons Park and at the Stables Gallery.

ALONG THE GREEN CHAIN

Created in 1977 to connect a chain of green spaces across four London boroughs, the Green Chain now includes nearly 300 such spaces, linked via 40 miles of footpaths connecting Thamesmead and Erith in the east to Chislehurst and Crystal Palace. The chain links up scores of interesting places, just as worthy of exploration as those in the centre of London.

Along the Green Chain
EXPLORE CHARLTON HOUSE GARDENS

Charlton House is a listed Jacobean mansion, built for Sir Adam Newton, Dean of Durham, and completed in 1612. Parts of it are sometimes attributed to architects John Thorpe, Norman Shaw and Inigo Jones.

The house is now owned by Greenwich Council, and though much is closed to the public, part of it is a lending library, and the grand gardens remain open, with carefully maintained lawns, a walled Peace Garden and even a ha-ha. The café in the central hall is open on weekdays.

www.charlton-house.org
Charlton Road, SE7 8RE
Charlton railway station

Along the Green Chain
SWIM IN CHARLTON LIDO

Charlton Lido is a 50-metre outdoor heated pool on the edge of Hornfair Park, originally opened in May 1939 as part of the expansion of London swimming pools which created Parliament Hill, Victoria Park and Brockwell Park Lidos.

After closure in 1989, Charlton Lido was the centre of community campaigns which opened it intermittently in the following years. The future now looks bright as the pool was reopened in 2013 thanks to a £2 million refurbishment.

www.better.org.uk
Hornfair Park, Shooters Hill Road, SE18 4LX
Charlton railway station

Along the Green Chain
HAVE TEA AT OXLEAS WOOD CAFE

Near the top of Shooters Hill, the popular little Oxleas Wood Cafe trades on good service, an unfussy menu and panoramic views over the parkland of Oxleas Meadows towards the Kent borders.

It sits on the edge of Oxleas Wood, which connects to Castle Wood, Jack Wood and Shepherdess Wood and is more than 8,000 years old.

www.oxleaswood.com
Shooters Hill, Greenwich, SE18 3JA
Falconwood railway station

Along the Green Chain
WATCH THE BIRDS AT MOTTINGHAM TARN

Mottingham Tarn, a hidden lake and nature reserve, once stood within the grounds of Eltham Lodge, a seventeenth-century house on the Eltham Palace estate.

The tarn is home to a range of wildfowl, and a great place to spot Canada geese, tufted and Mandarin ducks, coots and moorhens. There is also a colony of pipistrelle bats.

www.thetarn.org
Court Road, Mottingham, SE9 5AQ
Mottingham railway station

WALK BY THE QUAGGY IN CHINBROOK MEADOWS

Where once the River Quaggy was close to being lost, relegated to concrete culverts and subterranean tunnels, it has been coaxed back out into the open air as a normal river.

A project to reinstate the Quaggy in Chinbrook Meadows was completed in 2002, since when it has boasted a marshy habitat with reed beds, wild flowers and a board walk. The Meadows are also home to the Tutu Peace Garden, named after Archbishop Desmond Tutu who lived nearby in the 1970s.

Chinbrook Meadows, Amblecote Road, SE12
Grove Park railway station

GO DINOSAUR HUNTING AT CRYSTAL PALACE PARK

Victorian sculptor Benjamin Waterhouse Hawkins was commissioned to build the first dinosaur sculptures in the world, pre-dating Charles Darwin's *On the Origin of Species* by six years.

Now remembered as the world's first theme park, the park at Crystal Place still displays the models representing fifteen extinct species. Whilst modern scientists would quickly recognise anatomical errors, these have been retained for Victorian authenticity.

www.bromley.gov.uk
Thicket Road, SE19 2GA
Crystal Palace railway and overground station

VISIT BECKENHAM PLACE

A Palladian-style mansion built on the site of the ancient Manor of Beckenham around 1770, Beckenham Place is the creation of John Cator, a timber merchant and property developer responsible for the development of much of Blackheath.

It was admired by many, especially after a portico was added in 1778, and early visitors included Dr Samuel Johnson. Today, surrounded by a golf course, it retains a fading charm and is opened on Sundays by the passionate and engaging Friends of Beckenham Place Park.

www.beckenhamplaceparkfriends.org.uk
Beckenham Place Park, BR3 5BP
Beckenham Hill railway station

Weekend Tips

Eltham Palace (Court Yard, Eltham, Greenwich, SE9 5QE), a 1930s art deco conversion of Henry VIII's childhood home, is also on the Green Chain, and is a must-visit attraction for all Londoners.

AUGUST BANK HOLIDAY LONDON

Since 1965, Londoners have observed a public holiday in late August, marking the end of the summer with street festivals, barbecues, walks and an extra evening in the pub. Though the weekend often brings rain, there's something to do whatever the weather, with around a million people heading to the Notting Hill Carnival, and special events in museums, parks and communities around the capital.

TAKE A SPEEDBOAT ON THE THAMES

London Rib Voyages have been offering high-speed Thames cruises on board nippy rigid-inflatable boats since 2006. Powered by 630hp engines, the boats can reach speeds of up to 35 knots, and being much smaller than most cruisers are extra manoeuvrable.

Departing from a base in the shadow of the London Eye, a number of tours are available. The best option offers a trip to the Thames Barrier and back, taking in a 10-mile stretch of river.

www.londonribvoyages.com
London Eye Millennium Pier, South Bank, SE1 7PB
Waterloo tube and railway station

Weekend Tips

Walworth Road (SE17), near Burgess Park, has plenty of shops for barbecue supplies, but save room for jerk chicken with rice and peas and rum punch, seemingly the official foods and drinks of carnival.

DRINK AT THE KINGS ARMS

A pretty little pub on a street of humble early-nineteenth-century brick workers' cottages, The Kings Arms in Roupell Street, near Waterloo station, was once a funeral director's, before finding its niche as a friendly neighbourhood pub serving ale to thirsty locals.

It is almost always busy, but few customers mind having to spill onto the beautiful street outside, somehow spared by the bombs of the Blitz which obliterated large parts of the surrounding area.

25 Roupell Street, SE1 8TB
Waterloo tube and railway station

HAVE A BARBECUE IN BURGESS PARK

Whilst some London councils spurn barbecues, Burgess Park in Southwark actively encourages them, with designated barbecue areas around the lake.

This most tolerant of parks even has six permanent brick barbecues for the use of anyone able to bring their own grill, as well as picnic benches and concrete slabs to accommodate disposable barbecues.

www.southwark.gov.uk
Burgess Park, Albany Road, SE5
Elephant & Castle tube and railway station

ATTEND THE NOTTING HILL CARNIVAL

Europe's biggest street party takes to the streets of West London each August Bank Holiday weekend, with a family day on Sunday and a more festive full carnival parade on Monday, often attracting crowds of more than a million.

It has been taking place since the 1960s, when the first carnivals were organised to celebrate the culture of those who had arrived in London from the West Indies, at the same time diffusing racial tensions.

www.thenottinghillcarnival.com
Ladbroke Grove, W14
Lancaster Gate tube station

WATCH THE PANORAMA STEEL BAND COMPETITION

Held each year on the August Bank Holiday Saturday, the National Panorama Competition draws steel bands from around the country to get into the Caribbean spirit ahead of their performances at the Notting Hill Carnival later in the weekend.

The competition has been a warm-up for the carnival for over thirty years, echoing panorama competitions around the world. Typically it attracts up to 1,000 participants, keen to demonstrate their steel-pan expertise.

www.thenottinghillcarnival.com
Often at Emslie Horniman's Pleasance Park, Bosworth Road, W10 5EH
Westbourne Park tube station

SEE A SCARY FILM AT FRIGHTFEST

First organised by Paul McEvoy, Ian Rattray and Alan Jones at the Prince Charles Cinema in 2000, FrightFest has been held at various venues around Leicester Square since then, attracting horror fans to enjoy a scary film or two.

The festival usually takes place over the whole weekend, with numerous screenings all within the same cinema, and is now so popular that spin-off events have been organised around the country.

www.frightfest.co.uk
Leicester Square, WC2H
Leicester Square tube station

PICK BLACKBERRIES ON HACKNEY MARSHES

By the end of August, the fruit harvest is at its height, but you do not have to live in open countryside to find something tasty growing wild. Hackney and Walthamstow Marshes are just two places where it is possible to fill a basket among the blackberry bushes.

Patches of berries can be found all over the park, but particularly rich pickings can be found in the scrub between the football pitches and the canal.

Hackney Marshes, Homerton Road, E9 5PF
Hackney Wick overground station

AUTUMN

As autumn begins, events and street parties continue long into September, with the Totally Thames Festival, Open House London and the London Design Festival, before Halloween and Bonfire Night keep the party alive right through until November. As the clocks go back, London tends to retreat inside, but with Europe's best indoor arts and culture, food and drink in historic pubs and some of the world's best restaurants on offer, there is no chance of hibernation. Well-lit squares, parks and walkways throughout the city also continue to offer pleasant places to be outdoors, as long as a good coat, hat and scarf are on hand.

PIRATES' LONDON

From the sixteenth century to the eighteenth, the port of London was a hotbed for pirates, privateers and smugglers, and the notorious Mary Read and Edward Low were born and bred in the city. Support for privateering by English monarchs blurred the boundaries, keeping London at the heart of the industry for more legitimate sailors. Until 1700 all cases of piracy committed by British subjects or in the British colonies were heard in London, so captured pirates were dragged back to face trial and sentence. You can still get a flavour of the lives of London's pirates, real and imagined, at various places in the city.

FIND THE ORIGINAL SKULL AND CROSSBONES

The 'Jolly Roger' flag is one of the enduring symbols of the age of piracy. Legend has it that it was inspired by the skulls and bones which still stand atop the gateposts at St Nicholas's and St Luke's Church in Deptford.

The area is rich in maritime history, as the site of the shipyards which operated from the 1500s to the 1800s, and it is not beyond the realms of imagination that a pirate might have copied these gateposts for his emblem.

www.deptfordchurch.org
Deptford Green, SE8 3DQ
Deptford railway station

REMEMBER THE HANGING PIRATES OF ISLAND GARDENS

After being hanged at Execution Dock, the bodies of executed pirates were often tarred and strung up on a gibbet beside the Thames, as a warning to departing sailors of the price of piracy. One popular spot was Island Gardens at the tip of the Isle of Dogs.

Long before the foot tunnel connected Greenwich to Island Gardens, the pensioners of Greenwich Hospital hired out telescopes for visitors to catch a glimpse of the ill-fated pirates.

Saunders Ness Road, E14 3EB
Island Gardens DLR station

EXPLORE SAILORTOWN

Within the historic halls of the Museum of London Docklands, the Sailortown galleries recreate life in bustling Victorian Wapping. The exhibit is designed to reflect the winding lanes of Wapping between 1840 and 1850, and features a public house, lodging houses, a chandlery and even a wild-animal emporium.

Upstairs, a smaller gallery recreates the crowded waterfront wharves of eighteenth-century 'Legal Quay', where ships would have unloaded their cargo, and features an iron gibbet cage, once used to display the bodies of executed pirates.

www.museumoflondon.org.uk
Museum of London Docklands, West India Quay, Canary Wharf, E14 4AL
West India Quay DLR station

DRINK IN WAPPING'S PIRATE PUBS

On 23 May 1701, Captain William Kidd was brought to Execution Dock in Wapping to be hanged, guilty of piracy and murder. Not far away stood the ancient Town of Ramsgate pub and the Prospect of Whitby, both meeting places for pirates and smugglers.

This spot had been used for three centuries to put pirates, smugglers and mutineers to death. Legend has it that some pirates were chained to a post at the bottom of Wapping Old Stairs, and left to drown.

www.townoframsgate.co.uk
Town of Ramsgate, 62 Wapping High Street, Wapping, E1W 2PN
Wapping overground station

Pirates' London

SEE THE GHOST PIRATE SHIPS AT TOBACCO DOCK

Though the Tobacco Dock shopping centre in a listed warehouse in Wapping has stood virtually empty for decades, two pirate ships are still found beside it, originally built to entertain the children of expected shoppers.

The *Sea Lark*, a replica of a 330-ton tobacco and spice ship built at Blackwall Yard in 1788, and the *Three Sisters*, a copy of an eighteenth-century American-built merchant schooner captured by the Admiralty during the Anglo-American War, were to have been a floating pirate museum.

50 Porters Walk, E1W 2SF
Shadwell DLR and overground station

Pirates' London

PLAY PIRATES IN KENSINGTON GARDENS

For young pirates looking for fun in London parks, there are few better places than the Diana, Princess of Wales Memorial Playground in Kensington Garden. Inspired by the tales of Peter Pan, whose author J. M. Barrie lived nearby, it features a wooden pirate ship becalmed on a sandy beach, complete with palm trees and rope bridges.

It also boasts a sensory trail and a number of teepees, with ample seating and a café for adults.

www.royalparks.org.uk
The Broad Walk, Kensington Gardens, W2 4UH
Queensway tube station

Pirates' London

WALK THE DECKS OF THE *GOLDEN HINDE II*

In Elizabethan days there was a fine line between privateering and piracy. Francis Drake's first circumnavigation of the globe between 1577 and 1580 saw him capture a number of Spanish ships and their treasure, and on his return Queen Elizabeth I boarded the *Golden Hinde* at Deptford to bestow a knighthood on him.

The original *Golden Hinde* was kept as a museum for nearly a century before being broken up in the seventeenth century. The *Golden Hinde II*, a replica launched in 1973, is kept at St Mary Overie Dock.

www.goldenhinde.com
St Mary Overie Dock, Cathedral Street, SE1 9DE
London Bridge tube and railway station

Weekend Tips

Within Kensington Gardens, the Orangery at Kensington Palace (Kensington Gardens, W8 4PX), originally built to house Queen Anne's fruit trees, serves breakfast, lunch and afternoon tea.

THE HOUSES OF HAMPSTEAD

Once a sleepy village some way north of London, Hampstead's moment arrived in the late seventeenth century, when wealthy Londoners began to relocate after the twin blows of the Great Plague of 1665 and the Great Fire of 1666. As the eighteenth century dawned, Hampstead's wells were advertised for the medicinal value of their chalybeate waters, and it became a spa village. Its fortunes only increased with Victorian expansion, and the large houses which had come to dominate the hillside increased in number. Today, there are as many as ever, and they sell for millions of pounds. Some of the more famous houses are open to the public, and are well worth a visit.

The Houses of Hampstead
STEP INTO ERNÖ GOLDFINGER'S HOME

The family home of architect Ernö Goldfinger was built in the 1930s. The subject of huge controversy, it so annoyed neighbour Ian Fleming that he used Goldfinger's name for a James Bond villain. Today it is heralded as an interesting example of its style and is open to the public.

Inside the neat little house, home to the family until 1994, everything remains in situ, with children's toys in the upstairs nursery, art on the walls and even a Christmas pudding in the kitchen cupboard.

www.nationaltrust.org.uk
2 Willow Road, Hampstead, NW3 1TH
Hampstead Heath overground station

The Houses of Hampstead
DISCOVER FENTON HOUSE

A fantastic seventeenth-century merchant's house, occupying one of the best sites on top of Windmill Hill, Fenton House has managed to survive almost completely intact, with its large and interesting garden, for more than three centuries.

One of only a few original houses in the area, Fenton is now owned by the National Trust, having been left to them by Lady Katherine Binning in 1952. It is a great place to poke around, especially when the rooftop balcony is open, offering spectacular views.

www.nationaltrust.org.uk
Hampstead Grove, Hampstead, NW3 6SP
Hampstead tube station

The Houses of Hampstead
ADMIRE CONSTABLE'S VIEW FROM LOWER TERRACE

The artist John Constable often rented houses in Hampstead during the summer months, and painted a number of studies of clouds over the heath. Between 1821 and 1822, he rented 2 Lower Terrace. It was here that his daughter Isabel was born and it was also where he painted *View of Lower Terrace, Hampstead*, depicting the neighbouring houses, numbers 3 and 4.

The painting now hangs in a gallery at the V&A Museum in South Kensington.

collections.vam.ac.uk
2 Lower Terrace, NW3 6RE
Hampstead tube station

VISIT KENWOOD HOUSE

Surely Hampstead's grandest house, originally constructed in the early seventeenth century and remodelled by William Murray, the 1st Earl of Mansfield, Kenwood sits in landscaped gardens on the northern reaches of Hampstead Heath.

After being saved from developers, the house was left to the nation by Guinness heir the 1st Earl of Iveagh in 1927, along with its art collection, including works by Rembrandt, Van Dyck, Constable and Turner. It remains in the care of English Heritage.

www.english-heritage.org.uk
Hampstead Lane, Hampstead, NW3 7JR
Highgate tube station

PLAY SKITTLES AT THE FREEMASONS ARMS

Though the upstairs was smartened to meet upmarket local tastes some time ago, tucked away in the cellar of the Freemasons Arms is a traditional skittle alley, one of only a handful remaining in London.

There was formerly a skittle alley here in a garden outhouse built in 1819, and the current alley was installed in 1933 when the pub was rebuilt. It is now home to the Hampstead Lawn Billiards and Skittles Club, and can be booked for a game by amateurs.

www.londonskittles.co.uk
Downshire Hill, Hampstead Heath, NW3 1NT
Hampstead Heath overground station

EXPLORE THE HILL GARDEN AND PERGOLA

On the quieter western slopes of Hampstead Heath, the Hill Garden is a magical place for an aimless wander, with views across north London. The garden and its Edwardian terraces, gazebos and rose pergola were commissioned by soap magnate Lord Leverhulme, as a crowning glory to his home The Hill.

However, it was twenty years before the ambitious project was completed, shortly before Leverhulme's death in 1925. The house was then owned by Baron Inverforth and renamed Inverforth House, before passing into public ownership in 1960.

www.cityoflondon.gov.uk
North End Way, Hampstead, NW3 7EX
Hampstead tube station

Weekend Tips

There are some great pubs in Hampstead, including The Holly Bush (22 Hollymount, NW3 6SG) and the Duke of Hamilton (23–25 New End, NW3 1JD).

EAT AT THE BUTTERY CAFÉ AT BURGH HOUSE

Found within Burgh House, a listed Queen Anne building which now houses the Hampstead Museum, the Buttery Café also spills out into the leafy gardens.

The café is known for its coffees, cakes and afternoon teas, but is also fully licensed and offers a daytime menu of brunches and home-cooked seasonal British and European dishes, with a range to suit any appetite.

www.burghhouse.org.uk
New End Square, Hampstead, NW3 1LT
Hampstead tube station

IMMIGRANT LONDON

A city founded either by Romans from the Apennine Peninsula, or Trojans from modern-day Turkey, depending on which creation myth you believe, London has never been without immigrants, and has always taken inspiration from them. The Romans were followed by the Vikings, the Saxons and the Normans, who all shaped modern London, and later arrivals brought culinary favourites such as fish and chips, ice cream and curry, while immigrants like Marc Isambard Brunel, Sigmund Freud and George Frideric Handel fashioned the engineering, intellectual and musical life of the city.

VISIT 19 PRINCELET STREET

Built in 1719 on what were then still green fields on the edge of the City of London, 19 Princelet Street was once home to the Ogiers, a Huguenot silk-weaving family who had fled Louis XIV's persecution in France. By 1869, many French émigrés were replaced in the area by Jewish people escaping the pogroms of Russia and Eastern Europe. A synagogue was added in the garden, which thrived for a century.

Today, the house is occasionally open as London's Museum of Immigration and Diversity, in an area now home to many people of Bengali heritage.

www.19princeletstreet.org.uk
19 Princelet Street, E1 6QH
Shoreditch High Street overground station

Weekend Tips

Visitors can sample some of the international culinary highlights of Brick Lane at the various Bengali restaurants at the southern end, and at Brick Lane Beigel Bake (159 Brick Lane, (E1 6SB) to the north.

EAT IN LONDON'S MINI KOREA

Though New Malden in Kingston upon Thames, one of the largest communities of Koreans in Europe, is London's real Little Korea, another even smaller one exists on St Giles High Street near Tottenham Court Road.

Here, a number of Korean and Japanese eateries cluster together in an inexplicable but gastronomically welcome row, with Assa at number 53, Seoul Bakery at 55, Po Cha at 56 and Woo Jung at 59. Stepping inside is like entering a tiny bit of Seoul.

St Giles High Street, WC2H
Tottenham Court Road tube station

EXPLORE THE SHRI SANATAN HINDU MANDIR

Completed in 2010, Ealing's Shri Sanatan Hindu Mandir is a Hindu temple which attracts thousands of visitors each year, covering a site of 2.4 acres and standing 20 metres (66 feet) tall.

The temple was constructed from Indian limestone and marble quarried in Rajastan and Gujarat, carved in India before being shipped to London and assembled by expert craftsmen over fourteen years.

www.svnuk.org
Ealing Road, Wembley, HA0 4TA
Alperton tube station

Immigrant London

STAND IN
WINDRUSH SQUARE

The docking of the MV *Empire Windrush* at Tilbury
in June 1948 brought 492 hopeful settlers from
Jamaica, a symbolic start to post-war immigration
to Britain. Though many arrivals already had
accommodation and work arranged, some were
housed temporarily in an old air-raid shelter under
Clapham Common.

They used the labour exchange in Coldharbour
Lane, and inevitably many chose to stay in the area,
with others arriving to join them, and Brixton
became known for its Caribbean community. Fifty
years later, Brixton's main central square was
renamed Windrush Square.

Windrush Square, Brixton Road, SW2 1JQ
Brixton tube station

SEE UNIQUE INTERIORS AT 575 WANDSWORTH ROAD

In 2010, the National Trust acquired the home of Khadambi Asalache, the exiled Kenyan-born poet and writer who later became a Treasury civil servant. It is open to the public by guided tour.

Asalache arrived in Britain in 1960 and bought the house in 1981. He began creating the beautiful Moorish-style fretwork now seen around the house to cover up a patch of damp, before adding twenty-five years' worth of highly decorative embellishments.

www.nationaltrust.org.uk
575 Wandsworth Road, SW8 3JD
Wandsworth Road overground station

TOUR THE JEWISH MUSEUM

First established in 1932 in Bloomsbury, the Jewish Museum moved to Camden in the 1990s, combining with the London Museum of Jewish Life to form the existing museum.

Among its various artefacts is a medieval Jewish ritual bath, recovered from a building site in the City, and there are carefully considered displays about the Jewish faith and the social history of Jews in London. The real highlights, however, are the smiling volunteers of all ages on hand to explain the meaning and context of the collection.

www.jewishmuseum.org.uk
Raymond Burton House, 129–131 Albert Street, NW1 7NB
Camden Town tube station

DANCE A CÉILÍ AT THE LONDON IRISH CENTRE

Opened in 1955 to offer support to Irish immigrants arriving in London during Ireland's 'lost decade', Camden's London Irish Centre continues to be a focal point for the Irish community and Irish culture in London.

The centre holds regular céilí dances in the Kennedy Hall, its vibrant social centre. They are open to all, offering vigorous dancing to a live band, and a chance to enjoy this bastion of Irish culture and folk music in its element.

www.londonirishcentre.org
50–52 Camden Square, NW1 9XB
Camden Road overground station

SPORTING LONDON

As the capital city of the country whose citizens invented football, rugby, cricket, hockey and many of the world's greatest games, it should hardly be a surprise that London has a rich sporting pedigree. It was the home of the world's first indoor swimming club, opened in 1742 in Whitechapel, and of the world's first mountaineering club, founded in 1857. The stage for the Wimbledon Championships, and the venue for the 1966 FIFA World Cup Final, more recently London became the only city to have hosted the Olympic Games three times. Londoners continue to express a love of sports, with events which take place in their city screened around the globe.

VISIT THE HOME OF RUGBY

Originally built in 1907 on a site that had once been a cabbage patch, Twickenham is the largest rugby union stadium in the UK with a capacity of 82,000, and the home of the England team.

The stadium also houses the World Rugby Museum, and as well as viewing some of the 10,000 or so items, keen fans can take a tour which includes the royal box, players' tunnel and president's suite, along with the England players' changing room.

www.rfu.com/twickenhamstadium
Whitton Road, Twickenham, TW2 7BA
Twickenham railway station

LEARN THE HISTORY OF TENNIS AT WIMBLEDON

Though it draws most attention for two weeks in June and July, the All England Lawn Tennis Club hosts tennis matches all year round, and is also home to the Wimbledon Lawn Tennis Museum.

The museum contains items from throughout the history of the club, from 1877 to the present day, together with a collection tracing the history of tennis all the way back to its origins, with memorabilia dating from as early as 1555.

www.wimbledon.com
Church Road, Wimbledon, SW19 5AE
Wimbledon Park tube station

ATTEND A GAME AT CHAMPION HILL STADIUM

South London's Dulwich Hamlet have been playing at Champion Hill in East Dulwich since 1931, and during the 1948 Olympics the ground was even the venue for matches between participating nations.

Though the ground no longer draws the crowds of 20,000 it saw in its heyday, when it was one of the largest amateur grounds in England, it remains an atmospheric place. Loyal fans are accommodating to visitors who show up at the turnstiles.

www.dulwichhamletfc.co.uk
Edgar Kail Way, East Dulwich, SE22 8BD
East Dulwich railway station

PLAY PITCH AND PUTT IN MORDEN PARK

Though the manicured greens and fairways of Kent and Surrey suggest otherwise, you do not have to be a millionaire with a sports car full of expensive kit to be a London golfer, and at Morden Park you can enjoy a nine-hole pitch-and-putt course for under £10.

The park covers over 100 acres of what was once the gardens and estate of eighteenth-century Morden Park House. Golfers can cool off afterwards with a swim at neighbouring Morden Park Swimming Pools.

www.merton.gov.uk
Epsom Road, Morden, SM4 5QU
Morden South railway station

Sporting London
SWIM LIKE AN OLYMPIAN AT THE AQUATICS CENTRE

For two weeks in summer 2012, London was the centre of world sport as more than 10,000 athletes descended on the city for the Games. The pools which witnessed many of the most exciting moments are now open for the public to enjoy.

Designed by architect Zaha Hadid, the Aquatics Centre has two 50-metre Olympic pools and one 25-metre diving pool, and as part of the legacy of the games, entry is kept to the average price of a swim in an ordinary east London pool.

www.londonaquaticscentre.org
Queen Elizabeth Olympic Park, E20 2ZQ
Stratford tube, DLR, overground and railway station

Sporting London
WATCH CRICKET ON THE WORLD'S OLDEST PITCH

Matches have been played on Mitcham Cricket Green since 1685, and it is still the venue for regular fixtures of Mitcham Cricket Club, making it the world's longest continuously used ground.

Admiral Nelson once watched Mitcham play matches here, and England cricketer and local pub landlord James Southerton ran out W. G. Grace during a match in 1875. Many Mitcham players have gone on to great things, including England fast bowler Tom Richardson and wicket keeper Herbert Strudwick.

Mitcham Cricket Green, Mitcham, CR4
Mitcham Junction railway station

Sporting London
TAKE A TOUR OF THE EMIRATES STADIUM

London's most successful football team was founded in Woolwich in 1886 as a sports club for workers at the Royal Arsenal, and moved to north London in 1913.

In 2006, Arsenal Football Club relocated from the old ground at Highbury to a brand new 60,000-seater stadium on Hornsey Road known as the Emirates Stadium. Regular tours are available, with either a self-guided option or a 'Legends' tour led by an Arsenal player, both of which finish in the Arsenal Museum.

www.arsenal.com/tours
Hornsey Road, N5 1BU
Arsenal tube station

Weekend Tips

Halfway between Morden Park and Mitcham Cricket Green, Morden Hall Park is a pleasant National Trust property with a good tea room (Morden Hall Park, Morden Road, SM4 5JD).

BOOZY LONDON

Drink is not a modern vice, and for at least 4,000 years people in Britain have enjoyed a tipple. Around 2,000 BC, drinking was so important to the Neolithic Beaker People that they were buried with their beer mugs, some of which have been dredged from the Thames, and the Romans brought amphorae of wine just to make sure, before establishing vineyards around the country. Later, the northern European Angles and Saxons ensured that beer returned to vogue, but by the eighteenth century, gin was the city's drink of choice, with the 'gin craze' inspiring the public outrage immortalised in Hogarth's depiction of *Gin Lane*. Drinking is still as popular as ever in London, with a pub on nearly every corner.

AMBLE AMONG THE VINES IN GODSTONE VINEYARD

On the gentle south-facing slopes of the North Downs, Godstone Vineyard was planted by the Deeley family in 1985, and the first wines were bottled in 1988.

The vineyard covers 50 acres of sunny Surrey countryside, where the chalky free-draining Upper Greensand soil being ideal for vine-growing. As well as a chance to see the vines up close, the vineyard also offers wine tasting, and good food in its popular cafeteria.

www.godstonevineyards.com
Quarry Road, Godstone, RH9 8DQ
Caterham railway station

BUY WHISKIES AT MILROY'S OF SOHO

Milroy's started life as a wine merchant run by the Milroy brothers, but as the market for single malt whisky developed, the brothers established themselves as London ambassadors.

The Milroys regularly drive to Scotland to source whiskies for their range, which includes anything from Johnnie Walker miniatures at about £2.50 each to a fifty-year-old Highland Park at around £10,000 a bottle.

www.milroys.co.uk
3 Greek Street, W1D 4NX
Tottenham Court Road tube station

DRINK AT THE COACH AND HORSES

A pub whose name became synonymous with the Soho drinking culture of the 1960s and '70s, the Coach and Horses prides itself on being the West End's best-known pub, perhaps partly thanks to 'London's rudest landlord' Norman Balon, who retired in 2006 after sixty years' service.

The pub has changed little since it was made famous by its associations with former punter and career alcoholic Jeffrey Bernard, and also with the raucous *Private Eye* dinners held upstairs. It continues to attract Soho characters and is a fine place for a drink.

www.thecoachandhorsessoho.co.uk
29 Greek Street, W1D 5DH
Leicester Square tube station

Boozy London

TASTE WINES AT VINOPOLIS

Opened in 1999 by wine merchant Duncan Vaughan-Arbuckle, Vinopolis is a 2.5-acre wine theme park beneath a set of Victorian railway arches a short distance from Borough Market.

Vinopolis provides interactive displays and plenty of information about the wines on offer, a chance to taste them and other alcoholic beverages, as well as food and lots of water.

www.vinopolis.co.uk
1 Bank End, SE1 9BU
London Bridge tube and railway station

Weekend Tips

Other great pubs near the Pride of Spitalfields include The Carpenter's Arms (73 Cheshire Street, E2 6EG), The Royal Oak (73 Columbia Road, E2 7RG) and The Dove (24–28 Broadway Market, E8 4QJ).

Boozy London

BROWSE AT GERRY'S WINES & SPIRITS

Claiming to have the UK's largest selection of spirits and liqueurs, Gerry's Wines & Spirits on Old Compton Street is a Soho institution, with an unrivalled range of interesting and unusual drinks, each labelled with a hand-written description.

Gerry's was founded in 1984 by Greek Cypriot Michael Kyprianou, who had begun his career bottling wines at another Old Compton Street off licence, Delmonico's. The shop took its name from his former business partner, Gerry, who left after six months.

www.gerrys.uk.com
74 Old Compton Street, Soho, W1D 4UW
Piccadilly Circus tube station

Boozy London

HAVE A PINT AT THE PRIDE OF SPITALFIELDS

It is hard to imagine a more genuine East End boozer than the Pride of Spitalfields on Heneage Street. Its clientele is as diverse as you might expect in an area home to ageing cockneys, a large Bangladeshi community and a set of trendy east London types.

It has been here since the mid-nineteenth century and, like most locals, claims to have been a haunt of Jack the Ripper. It was also the target of a petrol bomb attack in 2003, but if you visit on a quiet Sunday evening you will find nothing scarier than a sleepy curled-up cat.

3 Heneage Street, Spitalfields, E1 5LJ
Aldgate East tube station

WALK THROUGH THE OLD TRUMAN BREWERY

Once one of the largest breweries in the world, the Truman Brewery on Brick Lane was established as the Black Eagle Brewery around the time of the Great Fire of London, as builders started to use land outside the City more intensively.

Though the brewery closed in 1989, the buildings are still a dominant presence on Brick Lane, with various bars, shops and restaurants, and two Sunday markets making use of the old premises.

www.trumanbrewery.com
Brick Lane, E1 6QL
Shoreditch High Street overground station

REVOLUTIONARY LONDON

The nineteenth century brought new political freedoms to ordinary citizens in Britain and this, combined with London's position as capital of the Empire and a new atmosphere of philosophical and scientific inquiry, made it the place to be for foreign political activists, refugees and political thinkers, often persecuted in their home countries. The promise of free access to information was also a powerful draw, with the British Library Reading Room attracting political thinkers as diverse as Karl Marx, Sun Yat-sen, Mahatma Gandhi, Lenin and Mohammad Ali Jinnah, keen to learn from one of the most important bodies of knowledge in the history of the world.

SEEK BERNARDO O'HIGGINS IN RICHMOND

Richmond upon Thames might not seem like a revolutionary outpost, but Bernardo O'Higgins wasn't a particularly ordinary freedom fighter.

The son of an Irish-born Spanish officer who became governor of Chile, Bernardo was a key figure in the independence fight against the Spanish government, and became independent Chile's first head of state in 1818. A statue of him stands in O'Higgins Square, not far from where he lived at 2 The Vineyard when a student.

O'Higgins Square, TW9
Richmond tube, overground and railway station

Weekend Tips

Those without time to travel to Ealing should note that Hồ Chí Minh also worked at the Carlton Hotel in Haymarket and is commemorated by a plaque on the New Zealand High Commission (80 Haymarket, SW1Y 4TQ).

EAT AT THE DRAYTON COURT HOTEL

In 1911, the man who would later become Vietnamese communist leader Hồ Chí Minh took a job on a French ship, a decision that eventually brought him to London where he worked in the kitchens of the Drayton Court Hotel in Ealing.

Following education in France and the Soviet Union, Hồ returned to Vietnam in 1941, founding communist independence movement Viet Minh, and adopting the name by which he is now known, Hồ Chí Minh or 'Bringer of Light'.

www.draytoncourtlondon.co.uk
2 The Avenue, W13 8PH
West Ealing railway station

FIND LATIN LIBERATORS IN BELGRAVE SQUARE

Beside a statue of Christopher Columbus, who first took Europeans to South America, standstatues of two liberators in Belgrave Square.

A 1974 bronze of Simón Bolívar commemorates a man involved in liberation struggles across South America, who came to London in 1810 to seek British support. The other, by Juan Carlos Ferrero, is of 'The Liberator' José de San Martín, who helped free Argentina, Chile and Peru from Spanish influence and was exiled in London in the 1820s.

Belgrave Square, London, SW1X 8NS
Hyde Park Corner tube station

Revolutionary London
SPOT EMMELINE PANKHURST IN WESTMINSTER

Emmeline Pankhurst died on 14 June 1928, just weeks before the Representation of the People Act extended the right to vote to all women aged over twenty-one, for which she had been campaigning for forty years.

Such was her importance as a figurehead for the suffragettes that, by 1930, a statue of Pankhurst had already been erected in Victoria Tower Gardens, using funds raised by the Women's Social and Political Union and unveiled by Prime Minister Stanley Baldwin.

Victoria Tower Gardens, Millbank, SW1P 3JA
Westminster tube station

Revolutionary London
EXPLORE LENIN'S LONDON

Vladimir Lenin first came to London in April 1902, bringing his *Iskra* newspaper, which he edited from an office at what is now the Marx Memorial Library in Clerkenwell Green. He also made use of the British Museum Reading Room.

Lenin visited London six times between 1902 and 1911, holding the 2nd Congress of the Russian Social Democratic Labour Party in a chapel off Tottenham Court Road in 1903, and enjoying walks on Primrose Hill.

Begin at 37a Clerkenwell Green, EC1R 0DU
Farringdon tube and railway station

Revolutionary London
AVOID INSURRECTION IN SPA FIELDS

Though they are now a relaxing haven of rounded grass mounds and flower beds, in the winter of 1816 Spa Fields were a hotbed of revolution, as followers of land reformer Thomas Spence met to call for parliamentary reforms.

At the first meeting Henry Hunt spoke to a crowd of around 10,000 and was nominated to deliver a petition to the government, but the second meeting got out of hand as the crowd decided to march on the Tower of London, looting a gun shop in Snow Hill en route.

Spa Fields, Skinner Street, EC1 1AA
Farringdon tube and railway station

Revolutionary London
VISIT MARX'S GRAVE

After being expelled from Cologne and Paris, in 1849 philosopher Karl Marx was exiled to London, where he lived and worked until his death in 1883. He was interred in a modest grave at Highgate Eastern Cemetery beside his wife, attended by only a handful of people.

By the 1950s, his ideas had had such an impact worldwide that scores were coming to the grave and a huge granite monument was added, topped with a great bronze of Marx's head.

www.highgatecemetery.org
Highgate Cemetery, Swain's Lane, N6 6PJ
Archway tube station

ITALIAN LONDON

Though the modern Italian community in London began to form in the early nineteenth century, people have been arriving from the Apennine Peninsula for as long as the city has existed. Indeed, the first commercial settlement was founded by an Italian empire on the Thames in 50 AD. London and Rome remained close via Catholic pilgrimage and later the aristocrats who took their grand tours to Venice and Rome and returned with a love of Italian art, architecture and archaeology. The unification of Italy in the early nineteenth century brought Italians to England in significant numbers, with political dissidents finding refuge in London. As numbers of Italians more than doubled in the industrial boom years, a Little Italy formed in Clerkenwell, and later in Soho.

SEE CANALETTO'S VENETIAN SCENES

Though he relocated to London for nearly ten years to be closer to the patrons who had purchased his works during their grand tours, Canaletto is best known for paintings of his native Venice, a pair of which hang at the National Gallery.

The Basin of San Marco on Ascension Day and *A Regatta on the Grand Canal* are among Canaletto's grandest works, featuring the city and the Palace of Doge Alvise Pisani in festive mood, with carnival costumes, ceremonial barges and processions.

www.nationalgallery.org.uk
Room 38, The National Gallery, Trafalgar Square, WC2N 5DN
Charing Cross tube and railway station

HAVE SOME COFFEE AT BAR ITALIA

A historic remnant of Italian Soho, Bar Italia was opened in 1949 by Lou and Caterina Polledri, when food rationing was still in place. This atmospheric and thriving little place is almost always open, with the third generation of Polledris serving its famous coffee from a veteran forty-year-old coffee machine.

It is known for its red-and-white Formica fittings and tiled floors, neon clock, walls adorned with black-and-white pictures and huge poster of Rocky Marciano, given by the boxer's wife after he died in a plane crash in 1969.

www.baritaliasoho.co.uk
22 Frith Street, Soho, W1D 4RF
Leicester Square tube station

Italian London

BUY BOOKS AT THE ITALIAN BOOKSHOP

Having been in Cecil Court for more than twenty years, the Italian Bookshop moved to Warwick Street in 2012 to join the European Bookshop, but it continues to offer the same wide selection of books for expatriate Italians and linguists alike.

The shop also offers translations of English works alongside those originally written in French, Spanish, Italian or German, as well as DVDs, CDs, children's books and other literature. The Italian bookshop is on the ground floor.

www.italianbookshop.co.uk
5 Warwick Street, W1B 5LU
Piccadilly Circus tube station

Italian London

FACE OFF WITH EMPEROR HADRIAN

Just inside the British Museum is a bust of Emperor Hadrian, originally from the Villa Adriana, his country residence at Tivoli.

Though Hadrian was from a Spanish family he was born in Rome, and served in the army and as governor of Syria before becoming Emperor in AD 117. He visited Britain in AD 122 when, as a result of recent revolts, he initiated the construction of Hadrian's Wall 'to separate Romans from barbarians'.

www.britishmuseum.org
The British Museum, Great Russell Street, WC1B 3DG
Tottenham Court Road tube station

Italian London

WALK IN THE ITALIAN GARDENS OF KENSINGTON

Thought to have been commissioned by Prince Albert as a gift to Queen Victoria, the Italian Gardens were not completed until 1861, the year he died. Their design is based on the gardens at the couple's holiday home, Osborne House on the Isle of Wight.

The gardens were built at the head of the Long Water, where the River Westbourne once flowed into Hyde Park, and feature fountains with Carrara marble basins, leading down to the Tazza fountain. The elaborate Pump House which once housed a steam engine to operate the fountains is now a pleasant seated shelter.

www.royalparks.org.uk
Kensington Gardens, London, W2 2UH
Lancaster Gate tube station

ATTEND A SERVICE AT ST PETER'S ITALIAN CHURCH

By the middle of the nineteenth century, about 2,000 Italians were settled in the slums around Clerkenwell, and St Peter's was opened on 16 April 1863 for all Roman Catholics in the community.

Designed by the Irish architect Sir John Miller-Bryson, it was based on plans drawn by Francesco Gualandi of Bologna and modelled on the Basilica of San Crisogono in Trastevere, Rome. At the time of its consecration, it was the first church in Britain in the Roman basilica style.

www.italianchurch.org.uk
136 Clerkenwell Road, EC1R 5EN
Farringdon tube and railway station

VISIT THE ESTORICK COLLECTION

Opened in 1998 to bring together works of art collected by American sociologist Eric Estorick and his wife Salome in the aftermath of the Second World War, the Estorick Collection of Modern Italian Art is situated in Northumberland Lodge, the former home of architect Sir Basil Spence.

The gallery's permanent collection features work by artists such as Futurists Umberto Boccioni and Carlo Carrà, founder of Metaphysical Art Giorgio de Chirico and sculptors Medardo Rosso and Emilio Greco.

www.estorickcollection.com
39a Canonbury Square, N1 2AN
Highbury & Islington tube, overground and railway station

Weekend Tips

For those wishing to experience more of Italian culture, the Istituto Italiano di Cultura di Londra (39 Belgrave Square, SW1X 8NX) hosts concerts, exhibitions and events, and also offers Italian language courses.

THE GENTLE BRENT

Immortalised by Sir John Betjeman as the 'Gentle Brent' in his poem 'Middlesex', the River Brent passes though nearly twenty miles of north and west London from its source at the confluence of Dollis Brook and Mutton Brook in Hendon to join the Thames at Brentford. Though it is often hemmed in by industrial and suburban landscapes, as soon as it flows beneath Western Avenue the Brent's banks make way for river meadows and grassland, given over to public parks and occasional golf courses. It is occasionally possible to think yourself in the country, whilst still safely within Greater London.

STROLL THE GARDENS AT SYON PARK

Set in 40 acres of grounds just across the river from Kew Gardens, Syon Park is one of London's last remaining grand private estates. At its heart, Syon House is home to the Duke of Northumberland.

Despite occasional changes such as remodelling by Robert Adam in the 1760s, the house has been home to the same aristocratic family for more than four centuries. Today, the house and garden are open to the public on Sundays, and on other days during the summer.

www.syonpark.co.uk
Syon House, Syon Park, Brentford, TW8 8JF
Syon Lane railway station

TOUR BOSTON MANOR HOUSE

Boston Manor House is a grand Jacobean house built for a young widow called Lady Mary Reade in 1623. It would have looked much the same when the Roundheads and Cavaliers fought the Battle of Brentford in 1642 at what would become nearby Syon Park, or when City merchant Colonel Clitherow entertained King William IV and Queen Adelaide.

The house is open to the public and has a fine park with a beautiful lake, ancient cedar trees and a popular weekend café in the Pavilion.

www.fobm.org.uk
Boston Manor Road, Brentford, TW8 9JX
Boston Manor tube station

WATCH FOR BATS BENEATH WHARNCLIFFE VIADUCT

Designed by Isambard Kingdom Brunel, and completed in 1837 to carry the Great Western Railway across the Brent, Wharncliffe Viaduct spans 270 metres (886 feet). It bears the coat of arms and name of Lord Wharncliffe, chairman of the committee who helped the GWR bill through Parliament.

The viaduct's impressive eight arches have become London's most popular roosting spot for bats. Though they are heavily protected and should not be disturbed, the furry flyers can often be seen darting over neighbouring Churchfields recreation ground at dusk.

Churchfields Recreation Ground, Manor Court Road, W7
Hanwell railway station

GET LOST IN THE MILLENNIUM MAZE

Planted with a labyrinth of 2,000 yew trees and opened in May 2000 as part of Ealing Council's celebrations, the popular Millennium Maze in Brent Lodge Park beside the River Brent is open daily.

The maze offers a few minutes of simple pleasure, challenging visitors to find their way among the hedges and rewarding them with views across the park from a raised central shelter.

Brent Lodge Park, Church Road, Hanwell, W7 3BP
Hanwell railway station

The Gentle Brent

MEET THE ANIMALS AT BRENT LODGE PARK

Affectionately known by locals as 'bunny park', Brent Lodge Park is home to a mini-zoo containing exotic birds, mammals, reptiles and insects from around the world. The animal centre also helps to connect local people with domestic animals such as sheep, goats, rabbits and birds.

In 2011, a butterfly house was opened, offering the chance to get up close with tropical species.

www.ealing.gov.uk
Church Road, Hanwell, W7 3BP
Hanwell railway station

The Gentle Brent

SEEK OUT OLD ST ANDREW'S CHURCH, KINGSBURY

As visitors walk north-west from Wembley Stadium, the seemingly endless urban sprawl is broken by the triple joys of the Welsh Harp Reservoir, Fryent Country Park and the wooded churchyard of Old St Andrew's Church, Kingsbury.

This tiny medieval church is the oldest building in Brent, now in the care of the Churches Conservation Trust. It features an exterior of rendered flint rubble which contains Roman bricks and tiles. Though access is by appointment only, it is an ageless haven of restful tranquillity.

www.visitchurches.org.uk
Old Church Lane, Kingsbury, NW9 8RU
Wembley Park tube station

The Gentle Brent

WALK THE SHORES OF THE WELSH HARP

An unexpected feature squeezed between the M1 and urban Wembley, Brent Reservoir was created in the 1830s by damming the River Brent and the Silk Stream, little more than brooks here, to feed the Grand Union Canal.

Immortalised in a music hall song as 'The Jolliest Place That's Out', it is known as the Welsh Harp after a long-closed public house. The Welsh Harp Open Space is a popular park, from where visitors watch sailing boats, and spot rare birds from its bird hides.

www.brent.gov.uk
Birchen Grove, NW9 8SA
Wembley Park tube station

Weekend Tips

The Capital Ring walking route links Syon Park to Boston Manor, Wharncliffe Viaduct and Brent Lodge Park for a pleasant day's walk (see page 69). Kingsbury and the Welsh Harp are a short walk from Wembley Park station.

ENGINEERS' LONDON

As the centre of an empire that led the Industrial Revolution, London was the engineering capital of the world throughout the Victorian age, at the cutting edge of innovation and invention. Great engineers such as Isambard Kingdom Brunel, Thomas Crapper, James Watt, Robert Stephenson, Thomas Telford, Sir Joseph Bazalgette, Sir Barnes Neville Wallis and Guglielmo Marconi have all walked the streets of London at one time or another, finding inspiration in a city that has always been at the forefront of engineering.

Engineers' London
SEEK THE ENGINEERS AT KENSAL GREEN CEMETERY

Some of the greatest engineers of the Victorian era are found at Kensal Green Cemetery.

Established in 1832, it is the resting place of Sir Marc Isambard Brunel and his son Isambard Kingdom Brunel, two of the greatest names of the industrial age, but also of lesser-known greats such as John Braithwaite, inventor of the first steam fire engine, gunsmith Charles William Lancaster and railway engineer John Edward Errington.

www.kensalgreencemetery.com
Harrow Road, W10 4RA
Kensal Green tube and overground station

Engineers' London
ADMIRE PADDINGTON TRAIN STATION

Designed by Isambard Kingdom Brunel as the terminus for the Great Western Railway, Paddington station, completed in 1854, remains a cathedral of the industrial age. The scale of the interior is all the more impressive given that it is squeezed into a shallow cutting, penned in by the Paddington canal basin.

Brunel called upon Matthew Digby Wyatt to assist with the decorative ironwork, writing of his need to build a station 'in a great hurry'. Those who take the time to admire its grand arches are richly rewarded.

www.networkrail.co.uk
Praed Street, W2 1RH
Paddington tube and railway station

Engineers' London
RIDE THE WORLD'S FIRST UNDERGROUND RAILWAY

In 1863, the Metropolitan Railway opened the world's first underground railway between Paddington and Farringdon. Lit by gaslight and driven by steam trains, it carried 40,000 passengers on its first day.

The original line served seven stations, stopping at Edgware Road, Baker Street, Great Portland Street, Euston Square and King's Cross, taking eighteen minutes to complete the journey.

www.tfl.gov.uk
Paddington to Farringdon tube and railway stations

Engineers' London
WALK THE NORTHERN OUTFALL SEWER

Though it appears to be just a pleasant raised footpath and cycleway running through a long green space, the Greenway that links Bow and Beckton, passing through Stratford and West Ham, is an embankment containing Victorian engineer Joseph Bazalgette's Northern Outfall Sewer, designed to help save Londoners from the blight of cholera.

Passing alongside the London 2012 Olympic site, the public route ends just before Beckton Sewage Treatment Works, Europe's largest sewage works, constructed in the 1860s and today serving around 3.5 million people.

Wick Lane, London, E3
Pudding Mill Lane DLR station

DISCOVER CROSSNESS PUMPING STATION

Opened in 1865 as part of the redevelopment of the London sewers after several cholera outbreaks had killed up to 20,000 people a year, Crossness Pumping Station is a masterpiece of Victorian technology designed by engineer Sir Joseph Bazalgette and architect Charles Henry Driver.

Crossness is on a grand scale, with detailed Romanesque design and ornate cast ironwork. In 1985, a trust undertook to restore the Engine House and the engines to their original condition, an ongoing project which still allows for a number of open days each year.

www.crossness.org.uk
The Old Works, Thames Water STW. Belvedere Road. SE2 9AQ
Abbey Wood railway station

Engineers' London
FIND THE *GREAT EASTERN* SLIPWAY

At the time of completion, Isambard Kingdom Brunel's SS *Great Eastern* was the largest ship ever to have sailed. It was built at the Millwall Iron Works, but due to its size, neighbouring Napier Yard was also used.

The ship was built parallel to the Thames, which it was feared was not wide enough to launch it, and in 1858 it took numerous attempts to shift its 18,915 tons. A small section of the huge launch ramp is still visible beside Napier Avenue on the Isle of Dogs, not far from Masthouse Pier.

Napier Avenue, Isle of Dogs, E14 3QB
Mudchute DLR station

Engineers' London
LEARN ABOUT THE THAMES BARRIER

Opened in 1984 at a cost of £500 million, the Thames Barrier is one of the world's largest flood barriers, protecting nearly 50 square miles of central London. The river here is about 0.3 mile across, and the barrier is made up of ten steel gates, which rotate in order to control the flow of water.

An information centre on the southern bank is open from Thursday to Sunday, with a café, an exhibition on the river's history and a working scale model of the barrier.

Thames Barrier Information Centre, 1 Unity Way, Woolwich, SE18 5NJ
Woolwich Dockyard railway station

Weekend Tips

Stop for tea and cake at the View Tube (The Greenway, Marshgate Lane, E15 2PJ) for great views of the engineering and architectural feats of the Olympic Park.

PERSPECTIVES ON LONDON

With an area of more than 600 square miles, and a population of over 8 million, it is hardly a surprise that it can be difficult to get the measure of London and understand how it fits together. Many spend their entire lives in the city without ever visiting huge swathes of it, and there is no one place within it from where its whole can be seen. However, there are many where you can attempt to get a sense of the scale of London, piecing it together place by place and view by view. Though it can be a bit expensive, only then can you really understand the city's enormity and beauty.

Perspectives on London
CANOE THE THAMES

Nowhere is it possible to feel more connected to the forces that shaped London than afloat on the tidal Thames in a canoe, and Moo Canoes, a small company founded by Katy Hogarth and Alfie Hatt, takes anyone with the inclination to get close to these murky waters.

As well as offering paddle-it-yourself canoe hire on the canals of east London from the base beside Limehouse Basin, Moo gives guided trips on the River Thames, often including dinner and after-dark canoeing.

www.moocanoes.com
30 Pinnacle Way, Limehouse Basin, E14 7PB
Limehouse DLR and railway station

Perspectives on London
ADMIRE THE VIEW FROM THE ARCELORMITTAL ORBIT

Standing proudly above the Queen Elizabeth Olympic Park, the ArcelorMittal Orbit was constructed for the London 2012 Olympic Games and designed by sculptor Sir Anish Kapoor and designer Cecil Balmond.

The tower, which contains a dual-level viewing platform offering truly stunning views over east and central London, bills itself as Britain's largest sculpture and is constructed from 2,000 tonnes of steel.

www.arcelormittalorbit.com
3 Thornton Street, Queen Elizabeth Olympic Park, E20 2AD
Stratford tube, DLR, overground and railway station

Perspectives on London
TAKE A LONDON HELICOPTER TOUR

Whilst helicopter rides over London might seem like the domain of billionaires, London Helicopter Centres have been offering tours to ordinary sorts for more than fifteen years, with up to ten trips a day leaving their base at Redhill Aerodrome just outside the M25, and prices starting at £150.

Trips last around thirty-five minutes, whisking passengers at 90 miles an hour over the North Downs, and then from Richmond Park over Westminster, the City of London and Greenwich, before returning to base.

www.london-helicopters.co.uk
Redhill Aerodrome, Redhill, RH1 5JY
Nutfield railway station

Perspectives on London
SEE ST PAUL'S FROM NUNHEAD HILL

A strategically placed bench in a corner of Nunhead Cemetery offers a peaceful place to sit and admire one of London's great clear views to St Paul's Cathedral, framed by trees, and surrounded by stone angels and memorials. Near here, Turner sat and painted *Distant View of London from Nunhead with the Dome of St Paul's and the Sun Breaking through Stormy Clouds*, now in the Tate Britain. It is not hard to imagine this spot as the artist saw it.

www.fonc.org.uk
Nunhead Cemetery, Linden Grove, SE15 3LP
Nunhead railway station

Perspectives on London
STAND ON THE TERRACE AT THE OXO TOWER

Once owned by meat-extract manufacturers Lemco, who designed the windows to get around planning rules and advertise Oxo stock cubes, the terrace at the Oxo Tower offers stunning panoramic views over the Thames. As well as an excellent restaurant and bar, there is also a small public viewing gallery, accessible for free at the base of the tower.

Ride the lift to the restaurant and bar, and ask to be directed to the viewing platform.

www.coinstreet.org
Oxo Tower Wharf, Bargehouse Street, South Bank, SE1 9PH
Blackfriars tube and railway station

Perspectives on London
LINGER ON THE GOLDEN JUBILEE BRIDGES

Designed by Lifschutz Davidson Sandilands and built for the celebrations of Queen Elizabeth II's Golden Jubilee, the Golden Jubilee Bridges are two 300-metre footbridges spanning the Thames between Charing Cross station and the South Bank, flanking Isambard Kingdom Brunel's Victorian Hungerford Bridge.

Each offers a spectacular panorama, with a fine view of the Houses of Parliament, the London Eye and County Hall from the south bridge, and the Savoy, the South Bank and St Paul's Cathedral from the north.

Hungerford Bridge and the Golden Jubilee Bridges, WC2N 6PA
Embankment tube station

Weekend Tips

The Ivy House (40 Stuart Road, SE15 3BE) in Nunhead is a short walk from the cemetery, whilst at the northern end of Hungerford Bridge, Gordon's Wine Bar (47 Villiers Street, WC2N 6NE) is exceptional.

CATCH THE CABLE CAR

Though some have questioned its low usage, and the fact that it connects little-visited parts of London that were already well connected, cynicism drifts away as the Emirates Air Line lifts passengers high above the river, offering spectacular views across Docklands.

This Thames cable car offers a great vantage point for the towers around Canary Wharf, the Millennium Dome, the lighthouse at Trinity Buoy and the Thames Barrier, with Maritime Greenwich, Shooters Hill and the Olympic Park all visible in the distance.

www.emiratesairline.co.uk
East Parkside, North Greenwich, SE10 0FR
North Greenwich tube station

POLITICAL LONDON

The city that is home to the Mother of Parliaments is still the political heart of Britain, and continues to draw politicians and future statesmen from around the world, just as it did when Mahatma Gandhi, John F. Kennedy and Jomo Kenyatta chose it as a place to study when young men. The restaurants of Westminster still bustle with the gossip of the day, albeit quieter since journalists' expense accounts have been reduced, as Britain's future leaders jostle for position at the bars of local pubs.

SEE HOGARTH'S *ELECTION*

A highlight of Sir John Soane's Museum at Lincoln's Inn Fields, a series of four paintings by William Hogarth satirises the notorious Oxfordshire election of 1754, which took place after a two-year campaign characterised by bribery and corruption.

The paintings cover a feast thrown to sway electors, the canvassing for votes at alehouses, ill and even dead electors being brought to the polling station and successful Tory candidates being chaired through the streets in triumph. Visitors must wait for a special showing by museum staff.

www.soane.org
13 Lincoln's Inn Fields, WC2A 3BP
Holborn tube station

STAY IN A HOSTEL THAT WAS ONCE LABOUR'S HQ

Found within a building known as John Smith house, the Safestay Hostel on Walworth Road was the headquarters of the Labour Party from 1981 until 1997, when the party took office after a landslide election.

Originally built in the late eighteenth century, this listed building still retains the name of the Labour leader who died in office in May 1994. Inside, it is a modern and functional hostel with rooms of varying sizes.

www.safestay.co.uk
144–152 Walworth Road, Elephant and Castle, SE17 1JL
Elephant & Castle tube and railway station

TAKE A GUIDED TOUR OF THE HOUSES OF PARLIAMENT

Tours of the historic Palace of Westminster are available on Saturdays throughout the year, offering the chance to visit the chambers of the House of Commons and the House of Lords, as well as Westminster Hall, the eleventh-century masterpiece that is the oldest remaining part of Parliament.

They also include a visit to the Queen's Robing Room, where she dresses before the State Opening of Parliament, and Central Lobby, where MPs meet their constituents. Thrifty visitors can book a weekday tour through their MP.

www.parliament.uk
House of Commons, SW1A 0AA
Westminster tube station

DRINK AT THE RED LION

There has been a pub on the site of the Red Lion in Westminster since 1434. Its location between the Houses of Parliament and Number 10 Downing Street means that it remains at the heart of political life, with MPs and journalists often drinking here.

Though the pub was rebuilt in 1900 and refurbished in 2014, when it was reopened by the Chancellor of the Exchequer, it is not hard to imagine customers such as Prime Ministers Winston Churchill and Clement Attlee crossing the threshold.

www.redlionwestminster.co.uk
48 Parliament Street, SW1A 2NH
Westminster tube station

Political London
VISIT THE CARTOON MUSEUM

Though the Cartoon Art Trust was formed in 1988 to establish a museum for exhibiting cartoons, it was not until February 2006 that the Cartoon Museum was formally opened in Little Russell Street, a few streets from the British Museum.

The museum's permanent collection mixes the light-hearted comic-book cartoons from titles such as the *Beano* and *Dandy* with the hard-hitting political satires of Gerald Scarfe, Martin Rowson and Steve Bell amongst others.

www.cartoonmuseum.org
35 Little Russell Street, WC1A 2HH
Tottenham Court Road tube station

Political London
VIEW PORTRAITS OF POLITICAL PEOPLE

The National Portrait Gallery contains some of the greatest portraits in history, and though politicians feature throughout the collection, Room 25 on the first floor is dedicated to the theme of Portraits and Politics.

This collection does change, but the room is often dominated by Sir John Everett Millais's portraits of the two great rivals of Victorian politics, William Ewart Gladstone and Benjamin Disraeli.

www.npg.org.uk
St Martin's Place, WC2H 0HE
Charing Cross tube and railway station

Political London
LISTEN TO TALKS AT SPEAKERS' CORNER

A centre for independent thought since the nineteenth century, Speakers' Corner, in the north-east of Hyde Park, was born when Chartists came together to protest the suppression of workers' rights. Since then it has attracted such notable characters as Karl Marx, William Morris, George Orwell and Tony Benn.

The right to gather here was enshrined in law in 1872, and every Sunday draws a crowd of speakers and listeners, in a tradition that keeps healthy political discourse at the centre of national consciousness.

Marble Arch, Hyde Park, W2 2EU
Marble Arch tube station

Weekend Tips

London's political heart is not very big, and the landmarks of government are best seen on foot. Many politicians also walk around Westminster now that use of ministerial cars has been cut back.

HIDDEN SOUTH BANK AND BANKSIDE

Though river traffic has declined, the stretch of the Thames between London Bridge and Westminster is still London's main artery. In the 1950s and 1960s, the building and expansion of the Southbank Centre drew people back to the river, as did the completion of the Queen's Walk between Tower Bridge and Lambeth Bridge in 1994. The opening of Shakespeare's Globe and Tate Modern in 1997 and 2000 reinvented the South Bank yet again, enticing thousands all year round, and though it can be hard to escape the crowds thronging the walkways, there are still a few hidden gems in the area.

FIND THE FERRYMAN'S SEAT

Hidden away down the side of a restaurant building overlooking the Thames, the Ferryman's Seat is an echo of an earlier London, part of a long-forgotten series of seats used by ferrymen who carried Londoners across and along the river prior to the opening of Westminster Bridge in 1750.

The seat is in Bear Gardens, an alleyway that remembers Bankside's history as home to the Beargarden, a bear-baiting ring popular with Londoners until the seventeenth century.

Bear Gardens, Bankside, SE1 9ED
London Bridge tube and railway station

SEE THE REMAINS OF THE ROSE PLAYHOUSE

When the Rose, brainchild of theatrical entrepreneur Philip Henslowe, was constructed in 1587, it was the first theatre south of the river. Though it was pulled down around 1606, its place in history is secure as the first theatre to stage a production of any of Shakespeare's plays.

Archaeologists uncovered its remains in 1989. Open days are held each Saturday to see the excavations, and occasional performances take place, whilst the nearby Globe Theatre helps give an idea of how it might have looked.

www.rosetheatre.org.uk
56 Park Street, SE1 9A
London Bridge tube and railway station

GAZE UP AT THE WINCHESTER ROSE

The medieval Bishops of Winchester had huge wealth and political influence thanks to their large estates, and as a sign of their power in the early thirteenth century built Winchester Palace in Bankside, then one of the largest and most important buildings in London.

Over the centuries the area was divided into tenements and warehouses as population and industry expanded, and in 1814 a fire exposed parts of the palace's stonework. The Rose Window from its Great Hall can still be seen on Clink Street.

www.english-heritage.org.uk
Clink Street, Southwark, SE1
London Bridge tube and railway station

DRINK AT THE BOOT AND FLOGGER

A few streets from the hustle and bustle of Borough Market, on a quiet back street, the Boot and Flogger is an atmospheric wine bar known for its wood panelling, comfortable leather armchairs and friendly staff. It has the air of a Victorian gentlemen's club, though it only opened in 1964.

Across the road is Cross Bones, an unconsecrated graveyard and final resting place for female prostitutes of Bankside, known colloquially as 'Winchester Geese', as their licences were issued by the Bishops of Winchester.

www.davy.co.uk
10–20 Redcross Way, SE1 1TA
London Bridge tube and railway station

WALK ON GABRIEL'S WHARF BEACH

The closest thing London has to a beach, at low tide a small stretch of sand is exposed on the Thames foreshore in front of Gabriel's Wharf on the South Bank.

The beach is particularly popular with sand sculptors, who create temporary pieces of art to the delight of passing tourists.

www.coinstreet.org
Gabriel's Wharf, 56 Upper Ground, South Bank, SE1 9PP
Southwark tube station

GO TO AN EXHIBITION AT THE HAYWARD GALLERY

Housed in a Brutalist building designed by Dennis Crompton, Warren Chalk and Ron Herron, the Hayward Gallery opened in 1968. It hosts a changing programme of exhibitions of modern or contemporary art, with a particular flair for installations and ground-breaking pieces.

The gallery is named after Sir Isaac Hayward, a Welsh miner's son who became leader of London County Council, and as Chairman of the South Bank Project sub-committee helped to ensure the building of the Southbank Centre.

www.southbankcentre.co.uk
Southbank Centre, Belvedere Road, SE1 8XX
Waterloo tube and railway station

WATCH THE SUNSET FROM THE *TAMESIS DOCK*

Clinging to the banks of the Thames just upstream from Lambeth Bridge, the *Tamesis Dock* is a converted 1933 Dutch barge once known as the *English Maid*. Now a pub and restaurant, it makes a pleasant place to watch the sun set over Millbank, with stunning views to Tate Britain and the Houses of Parliament.

It is possible that some of your shipmates will be guarding top secrets as the boat is moored between Thames House, the MI5 Headquarters and the MI6 buildings at Vauxhall Cross.

www.tdock.co.uk
Albert Embankment, SE1 7TP
Vauxhall tube and railway station

Weekend Tips

As well as a beach, Gabriel's Wharf has a number of independent cafés, restaurants, bars and shops which are worth a visit.

THE NORTHERN HEIGHTS

To the north of the City of London, hills rise at Hampstead and Highgate offering fine views of central London landmarks. Here, a sand-and-gravel ridge rests on a band of London clay which extends out towards Alexandra Palace, where its height drops off towards Salmons Brook and the River Lea. The ridge is popular with London walkers, many of whom make use of the disused railway tracks once earmarked for a 'Northern Heights' extension to the Northern line, which would have connected Alexandra Palace and Highgate.

The Northern Heights
SKATE AT ALEXANDRA PALACE

Opened in 1873 as a north-London twin to the Crystal Palace in Sydenham, Alexandra Palace is found on a hill between Muswell Hill and Wood Green, with fine views southward to central London.

The building most famous as one of the first homes of BBC Television has twice been virtually destroyed by fire, in 1875 and again in 1980 when a fire began during a jazz festival. Refurbishments saw the addition of an ice rink in 1990, which is open daily all year round.

www.alexandrapalace.com
Alexandra Palace Way, N22 7AY
Alexandra Palace railway station

The Northern Heights
EXPLORE HIGHGATE WOOD

Highgate Wood, 70 acres of ancient woodland on the edge of Highgate village, was once part of the Great Forest of Middlesex, a vast area filled with stags, boars and wild bulls later hunted by the Bishops of London who claimed it for their estate.

It has oak, holly and hornbeam trees, and is a haven for wildlife with over seventy species of bird, as well as squirrels, foxes and bats. Evidence of early habitation, both prehistoric and Roman, has been found.

www.cityoflondon.gov.uk
Muswell Hill Road, N10 3JN
Highgate tube station

The Northern Heights
GO SHOPPING IN HIGHGATE VILLAGE

In the Georgian era, Highgate was a small hilltop village on the outskirts of London, mainly serving travellers approaching from the north.

The village centre still retains a strong sense of that time, with eighteenth-century architecture and leafy streets. A pretty jumble of independent shops tumbles down Highgate High Street from the Prince of Wales and The Angel Inn pubs, including the Highgate Pantry, High Tea of Highgate and Highgate Contemporary Art.

Highgate High Street, N6 5HX
Highgate tube station

The Northern Heights
WATCH A SHOW AT JACKSONS LANE

Reopened in 1976 as a community centre and theatre space, Highgate's Jacksons Lane began life as a Wesleyan Methodist church, designed by local architect W. H. Boney.

The centre hosts a full programme of theatre, comedy, dance and other performance in its 160-capacity theatre, as well as courses, training and practice in its dance and rehearsal spaces. The café bar is popular with locals.

www.jacksonslane.org.uk
269a Archway Road, N6 5AA
Highgate tube station

WALK IN WATERLOW PARK

Often overlooked due to its proximity to Hampstead Heath and Highgate Woods, Waterlow Park comprises 26 acres of green space given to Londoners as a 'garden for the gardenless' by Sir Sydney Waterlow, along with his home Lauderdale House.

As well as the beautiful landscaped gardens and ponds, many come here to visit the house, a sixteenth-century mansion once home to Charles II's mistress Nell Gwyn. There is an arts and education centre which hosts regular performances, exhibitions and classes, and a tea room.

www.waterlowpark.org.uk
Highgate Hill, N6 5HG
Archway tube station

ADMIRE THE VIEW FROM PARLIAMENT HILL

Parliament Hill rises 98 metres (321 feet) above sea level in the south-east corner of Hampstead Heath, and is its focal point. Scores of visitors come whatever the weather to admire the unrivalled view to the Palace of Westminster, St Paul's Cathedral, Canary Wharf and the Shard.

The view is considered so important that the line from the oak tree east of the summit towards the Houses of Parliament is protected from obstruction by law.

www.cityoflondon.gov.uk
Hampstead Heath, NW5
Hampstead Heath overground station

DRINK AT THE FLASK, HAMPSTEAD

The Flask on Flask Walk stands on a site once occupied by a thatched cottage to which villagers came to buy flasks of spring water, said to have medicinal qualities, for threepence each. The water was sold throughout London.

When Hampstead was absorbed by an expanding city, the cottage was demolished and replaced in 1874 by the pub. Now run by Young's, it is a popular spot for a drink or meal after a walk on the heath, surrounded by lots of polished wood.

www.theflaskhampstead.co.uk
14 Flask Walk, Hampstead, NW3 1HE
Hampstead tube station

Weekend Tips

It is roughly four miles from Alexandra Palace to Hampstead, and much of that can be walked off the roads via the Parkland Walk, which follows the route of the original Northern Heights line.

WINTER

Whilst other parts of Britain fall quiet as winter approaches, London is still as lively as ever, with seasonal arts, culture, food and drink helping residents to stave off the desire to remain in their homes. The city that inspired Charles Dickens's *A Christmas Carol* is a fine place to celebrate the festive season, with special events in churches, museums, squares and galleries to combat the onset of the winter blues. As New Year dawns, celebrations and parades continue. London offers opportunities for great walks, with green spaces close to habitation allowing ramblers the chance to duck into a pub or café if a shower sets in, and plenty of interesting wintry views en route.

NORDIC LONDON

Nordic influences have been present in London since at least the ninth century, when Viking raids became frequent, and in 1017 the Dane King Cnut was crowned King of England in London, as head of an Anglo-Scandinavian empire which flourished until the Norman Conquest. As a result of geography, ties between London and the Nordic countries have always been close, and the foundation of seamen's missions by various Scandinavian nations in Victorian times was indicative of increased trade links. Today, Scandinavians continue to come to London to live and work, and Scandinavian bars, coffee shops and restaurants can be seen around the city.

TAKE A SAUNA AT THE FINNISH CHURCH

The Finnish church is more of a Finnish outpost than simply a church, with a hostel, cafeteria, library and shop all under one roof.

It was first established in 1875 as the Finnish Seamen's Mission, helping sailors who found themselves in the city, though the current building dates from 1955. One of the more unexpected features is a traditional Finnish sauna, considered a vital amenity for Finns abroad, open to the public from Tuesday to Sunday.

www.finnishchurch.org.uk
33 Albion Street, SE16 7HZ
Rotherhithe overground station

EXPLORE GREENLAND DOCK

Originally called Howland Great Wet Dock, Greenland Dock was renamed in 1725 after whalers from Greenland. They had boiling houses on the docks to produce oil from whale blubber, used in oil lamps, in soap and as an industrial lubricant.

In 1806, timber from Scandinavian and Baltic countries took over, hence Finland Quay, Helsinki Square and Baltic Quay. The Ship & Whale in Gulliver Street, an attractive pub that has been in existence since at least 1767, is one remaining link to the whaling trade.

Greenland Dock, Rotherhithe, SE16 7PQ
Surrey Quays overground station

TOUCH A ROCK SHAPED BY NORWEGIAN GLACIERS

A huge boulder from Norway stands to the west of Ranger's Lodge in Hyde Park. An inscription explains that it was worn for thousands of years by frost, running water, rock sand and ice until it obtained its present shape.

This war memorial was presented by the Norwegian navy and merchant fleet in 1978 in thanks for Britain's help during the Second World War, with the message thanking the British people because 'You gave us a safe haven in our common struggle for freedom and peace'.

www.royalparks.org.uk
Hyde Park, Westminster, W2 2UH
Hyde Park Corner tube station

Weekend Tips

If hunger strikes during a visit to the Finnish church, find treats at the on-site cafeteria and Finnish food shop.

Nordic London
DRINK AT THE NORDIC BAR

A Scandinavian basement bar on Newman Street, Nordic Bar has been serving food and drink from the icy north for over a decade, with Carlsberg, Tuborg and Icelandic Einstök beers and Nordic cheeses, seafood and köttbullar meatballs, alongside a range of cocktails.

As is to be expected, the interior involves plenty of wood, and there is also a ping-pong table and table football. The bar is particularly popular on Friday and Saturday nights, and enjoys celebrating Scandinavian festivals and events, either in-house or with big-screen sport.

www.nordicbar.com
25 Newman Street, W1T 1PN
Tottenham Court Road tube station

Nordic London
EAT AT SCANDIKITCHEN

Owned by husband and wife team Bronte and Jonas Aurell, whose mission is to help Londoners embrace the tastes of their native Denmark and Sweden, ScandiKitchen is a café and grocery store that offers great Scandinavian food.

It is found on Great Titchfield Street, just north of Oxford Street, where it opened in 2006 serving customers seven days a week, with a smörgåsbord of Nordic treats to eat in or take home.

www.scandikitchen.co.uk
61 Great Titchfield Street, W1W 7PP
Oxford Circus tube station

Nordic London
BROWSE BOOKS AT THE SWEDENBORG

Founded in 1810 to translate and publish the works of Swedish scientist, philosopher and visionary Emanuel Swedenborg, the small bookshop sells the complete works of Swedenborg, as well as works by other writers.

Swedenborg died in London in 1772 and was buried at the Swedish church in Shadwell. After the church closed in 1909 and was demolished, his remains were removed to Sweden by warship, where he was buried in Uppsala Cathedral.

www.swedenborg.org.uk
20–21 Bloomsbury Way, WC1A 2TH
Tottenham Court Road tube station

Nordic London
READ THE RUNES ON THE JELLING STONE

An exact replica of Denmark's ancient Jelling Stone sits in the grounds of the Danish Church in St Katharine's Precinct. The original was erected in Jelling by King Harald Bluetooth in the tenth century, in memory of his parents, and in celebration of having 'won for himself all of Denmark and Norway and made the Danes Christian'.

The stone is brightly painted, as the original would have been.

www.danskekirke.org
4 St Katharine's Precinct, NW1 4HH
Mornington Crescent tube station

DICKENS'S LONDON

Charles Dickens was in many ways the ultimate Victorian Londoner, rising from poverty to become one of the greatest writers of all time, which he did by getting beneath the skin of the city and understanding its people and their lives. While many were reluctant to examine its darker side, Dickens walked London's streets for 10 or 20 miles at a time, day and night, drinking in its pubs, observing ordinary lives and immortalising the places he saw in books which travelled around the world.

Dickens's London

WALK THE WALLS OF MARSHALSEA PRISON

In 1824, when his father was imprisoned for debt in Marshalsea prison, the twelve-year-old Charles Dickens was sent to work in Warren's Blacking Factory close to modern-day Hungerford Bridge. This haunted him for the rest of his life, inspiring *Little Dorrit*.

The prison stood beside the churchyard of St George the Martyr in Southwark, and memorials in the alleyway beside the churchyard gardens remind us that was where John Dickens was jailed. The church also featured in Dickens's work.

www.stgeorge-themartyr.co.uk
Beside St George's Churchyard, Borough High Street, SE1 1JA
Borough tube station

Dickens's London

CROSS ST SAVIOUR'S DOCK

The Thames Path crosses a small bridge across St Saviour's Dock, just east of Tower Bridge. At low tide the exposed mud looks as it must have done when Dickens immortalised it in *Oliver Twist*, as villain Bill Sikes fell to his death in 'Folly Ditch'.

St Saviour's was on the border of Jacob's Island, a notorious rookery (slum) where poverty and crime were rife. Dickens wrote of its 'wooden chambers thrusting themselves out above the mud and threatening to fall into it'.

St Saviour's Dock, London, SE1
London Bridge tube and railway station

Dickens's London

SEEK OUT THE OLD CURIOSITY SHOP

Spared by both the Great Fire of London and the Blitz, the Old Curiosity Shop, at 13–14 Portsmouth Street off Lincoln's Inn Fields, claims to be the inspiration for Dickens's novel of the same name.

Built in the 1560s – legend has it using the wood from old ships – the shop has been variously a dairy, a paper merchant, an antiques shop and more recently an upmarket shoe shop.

www.the-old-curiosity-shop.com
13–14 Portsmouth Street, WC2A 2ES
Holborn tube station

Dickens's London

VISIT THE CHARLES DICKENS MUSEUM

Number 48 Doughty Street was home to Charles Dickens from 1837 until 1839, and it was here that he completed *The Pickwick Papers*, *Oliver Twist* and *Nicholas Nickleby*.

Dickens's only surviving London home, it was opened as a museum in 1925. It contains an important collection of rare editions and items from his life including bars from Marshalsea prison, his writing desk and his four-poster bed.

www.dickensmuseum.com
48 Doughty Street, WC1N 2LX
Russell Square tube station

Dickens's London
DRINK AT THE LAMB

A beautiful pub a few streets from Doughty Street, The Lamb is reputed to have been a favourite of Charles Dickens. It retains its Victorian air, with plenty of wood panelling and rotating 'snob screens' to allow drinkers to hide while not seeing the bar staff.

The pub, originally built around 1729, was also once the venue for a date between Ted Hughes and Sylvia Plath.

www.youngs.co.uk
94 Lamb's Conduit Street, Bloomsbury. WC1N 3LZ
Russell Square tube station

Dickens's London
EAT AT SIMPSON'S-IN-THE-STRAND

Originally Samuel Reiss's Grand Cigar Divan, and later a chess club and coffee house, Simpson's-in-the-Strand found its niche selling traditional meaty English dishes during the second half of the nineteenth century. It was a favourite of Charles Dickens.

In its heyday, the restaurant attracted anyone who wanted to be seen in London society, including Prime Minister William Gladstone. It was also patronised by P. G. Wodehouse and Sir Arthur Conan Doyle, who used it in Sherlock Holmes's *The Adventure of the Illustrious Client*.

www.simpsonsinthestrand.co.uk
100 Strand, WC2R 0EW
Charing Cross tube and railway station

Dickens's London
FIND THE SITE OF 1 DEVONSHIRE TERRACE

Though Dickens requested that there be no memorial to his life other than his writing, a few do exist, and a panel on a busy corner of Marylebone Road and Marylebone High Street remembers his home from 1839 to 1851.

Here, at what was then 1 Devonshire Terrace, he wrote six of his most famous novels, *The Old Curiosity Shop*, *Barnaby Rudge*, *A Christmas Carol*, *Martin Chuzzlewit*, *Dombey and Son* and *David Copperfield*.

Ferguson House, 15 Marylebone Road, NW1 5JD
Baker Street tube station

Weekend Tips

For a fitting Dickensian meal, reserve Dickens's fireside seat at Ye Olde Cheshire Cheese (Wine Office Court, 145 Fleet Street, EC4A 2BU), where he would often sit and write.

SUBTERRANEAN LONDON

For nearly a hundred years from 1831 until 1925, London was the world's most populous city, the heart of empire and an industrial powerhouse that ruled the world. With available land and property at a premium, it is hardly surprising that Londoners decided to dig for the future, and the world's first underground railway opened in January 1863, the start of a subterranean trend driven by necessity. Where once the ground was fit only for the dead, modern London readily makes use of any available space, and basement bars, cafés, shops and offices thrive in the centre.

STAND ON LONDON'S DEEPEST PLATFORM

Though at 58.5 metres (192 feet) Hampstead is usually named as London's deepest tube station, this is partly because of the hill on top of it, and technically it is above sea level. In terms of proximity to the centre of the earth, the Jubilee line platforms at Westminster are much deeper.

At 32 metres (105 feet) below sea level, they are at the bottom of London's deepest-ever excavation. It is difficult to imagine Members of Parliament in Portcullis House, their £200m office block, all that way above.

www.tfl.gov.uk
Bridge Street, SW1A 2JR
Westminster tube station

Subterranean London
SEE GRAFFITI IN LEAKE STREET TUNNEL

Whilst elsewhere in the capital, graffiti is either illegal or semi-legal, in the 200-metre (219-yard) Leake Street Tunnel beneath Waterloo station it is actively encouraged.

Originally decorated by street-art-for-profit pioneer Banksy and twenty-nine other artists as part of the Cans Festivals in summer 2008, the tunnel is an ever-changing canvas for London's spray-can lovers, and each visit brings new artworks.

Leake Street, SE1 7NN
Waterloo tube and railway station

Subterranean London
FIND SETI I'S SARCOPHAGUS

Centrepiece for Sir John Soane's Museum, the sarcophagus of Seti I sits in its own subterranean 'Sepulchral Chamber'. Upon installation in Soane's grand house, it was the subject of a three-night party attended by a thousand people.

The sarcophagus evokes the joy and shame of the age of Victorian acquisition. Carved in one piece of perfect white stone with hieroglyphics inlaid in blue, it stood in Seti's tomb for thousands of years before being transported to London where the smog damaged it irreversibly.

www.soane.org
Sir John Soane's Museum, 13 Lincoln's Inn Fields, WC2A 3BP
Holborn tube station

Subterranean London
SIP TEA IN THE CRYPT OF ST MARTIN-IN-THE-FIELDS

A great little café beneath the eighteenth-century brick-vaulted arches in the crypt of of St Martin-in-the-Fields on Trafalgar Square, the Café in the Crypt is open daily. Afternoon tea is a particular highlight, served daily from 2 to 6 p.m.

The modern café was created as part of a £36-million restoration project by Eric Parry Architects, completed in 2008, which helped to sympathetically alter the Grade I listed church, designed in a neoclassical style by James Gibbs and completed in 1726.

www.stmartin-in-the-fields.org
Trafalgar Square, WC2N 4JJ
Charing Cross tube and railway station

DRINK AT THE CORK AND BOTTLE

Whilst from the outside the Cork and Bottle might look like an uninviting prospect, those who venture down the stairs into this Leicester Square institution of more than forty years are rarely disappointed.

The bar was established beneath a sex shop in the heart of theatre land in 1972 by Don Hewitson. Although the surroundings have changed, the bar is still just as it always has been, serving good food and wine to all comers seven days a week.

www.thecorkandbottle.co.uk
44–46 Cranbourn Street, WC2H 7AN
Leicester Square tube station

VISIT ALL HALLOWS BY THE TOWER

As is to be expected from one of London's oldest churches, there is a lot of history to be found at All Hallows by the Tower. A small museum in the crypt helps to connect the dots between 675 AD, when the church was founded, and today.

In fact, the museum goes back even further, from a Roman pavement found here in 1926, via a Saxon wheelhead cross and a register noting the marriage of US President John Quincy Adams, to the present day.

www.allhallowsbythetower.org.uk
Byward Street, EC3R 5BJ
Tower Hill tube station

WALK THROUGH GREENWICH FOOT TUNNEL

Opened in 1902 to help Isle of Dogs dock workers get to work from their homes south of the river, Greenwich Foot Tunnel was designed by civil engineer Sir Alexander Binnie, also responsible for Vauxhall Bridge and the first Blackwall Tunnel.

It is 371 metres (1,217 feet) long and roughly 15 metres (50 feet) deep, lined with 200,000 glazed white tiles. Eerie echoes and occasional drips from the ceiling add to its otherworldly atmosphere, which is at its height when deserted late at night or early in the morning.

www.fogwoft.com
Cutty Sark Gardens, SE10 9HT
Cutty Sark DLR station

Weekend Tips

The extra journey to Greenwich takes some time, so allow yourself an hour or so to wander the Old Royal Naval College, and take pie and mash at Goddard's (22 King William Walk, SE10 9HU).

HIGHLIGHTS
OF HACKNEY

Now an epicentre of London cool, Hackney was once open farmland producing food for Roman London, and it was not until Tudor City merchants started to build their grand houses here that the area saw its first growth spurt. The nineteenth century brought industrialisation and railways, which laid out the busy street plans later torn apart by the bombs of the Blitz. Immigrants from Turkey, the Caribbean, Cyprus and South Asia then arrived to fill post-war labour shortages, helping to make it one of the most ethnically diverse areas in the country. Though two decades of gentrification have literally changed the face of once down-at-heel Hackney, it has retained much of its individuality, and still has plenty of charm.

SWIM AT LONDON FIELDS LIDO

Saved from the bulldozer in 1990 and reopened in 2007, London Fields Lido is a 50-metre heated outdoor swimming pool that is now the pride of locals, who enjoy a dip in its warm waters all year round.

The pool retains much of its original 1932 charm, whilst being updated to a modern style. Prices remain low enough to appeal to all members of the community.

www.better.org.uk
London Fields West Side, E8 3EU
London Fields railway station

TAKE TEA IN HACKNEY'S OLDEST HOUSE

A rather unexpected feature to anyone unfamiliar with the history of urban Hackney, Sutton House's National Trust tea room might have been transported from the Home Counties.

The licensed café straddles the conservatory and library of this grand Tudor house, built in 1535, and spills over into the central courtyard, making it a fine place for a cuppa.

www.nationaltrust.org.uk
2–4 Homerton High Street, E9 6JQ
Hackney Central overground station

MEET THE ANIMALS AT HACKNEY CITY FARM

For more than thirty years, Hackney City Farm has been bringing the sights and sounds of the farmyard to a quiet corner of Hackney, teaching local children where their food comes from and hosting regular community events.

The farm occupies a site once the home of West's Brewery, and now home to pigs, goats, sheep, donkeys and other animals. They rotate time in Hackney with time on a farm in Kent, to ensure they do not get too jaded by urban surroundings.

www.hackneycityfarm.co.uk
1a Goldsmiths Row, E2 8QA
Hoxton overground station

GO SHOPPING IN BROADWAY MARKET

Though it has become increasingly gentrified, there is still something charming about Broadway Market, one of London's oldest Chartered Markets.

Each Saturday, stallholders arrive early with a wide range of stalls selling everything from vintage clothes to fruit and veg, in a regular market that has been run since the 1890s.

www.broadwaymarket.co.uk
Broadway Market, E8 4PH
London Fields railway station

VISIT THE HACKNEY MUSEUM

One of London's best local museums, the Hackney Museum is an engaging local history showcase of the people who have made the borough their home over the last 1,000 years.

It uses social history to try to tell the story of all the borough's residents, who make up 200,000 people from six continents, and speak more than 100 languages, as well as displaying interesting items such as the gravestone of the writer Daniel Defoe and Hackney's first fire engine.

www.hackney.gov.uk
Ground Floor, 1 Reading Lane, E8 1GQ
Hackney Central overground station

WATCH A SHOW AT THE HACKNEY EMPIRE

Constructed in 1901 to designs by theatre architect Frank Matcham, the Hackney Empire was a music hall, attracting favourites such as Charlie Chaplin, Marie Lloyd and Stan Laurel during its early years.

After brief periods as a TV studio and a bingo hall, the Empire reopened in the 1980s, and became a popular venue on the alternative comedy circuit, before celebrating its centenary with an ambitious programme of refurbishments. It now hosts a range of theatre, music and comedy events.

www.hackneyempire.co.uk
291 Mare Street, E8 1EJ
Hackney Central overground station

BUY BOOKS AT PAGES OF HACKNEY

A wonderfully compact independent bookshop on Lower Clapton Road, Pages of Hackney opened in September 2008 and has since become an important part of the local community.

Upstairs, nooks and crannies are packed with fiction, children's, political, environment, art, cookery and second-hand books, whilst the basement gallery doubles as a space for regular events and exhibitions.

www.pagesofhackney.co.uk
70 Lower Clapton Road, E5 0RN
Hackney Central overground station

Weekend Tips

Broadway Market is the culinary centre of Hackney, even when the market is not taking place, with plenty of restaurants and cafés for different budgets. Frizzante is the award-winning café restaurant at Hackney City Farm.

LIONS OF LONDON

It is not clear when the lion began to be used as a symbol for England, but the association was certainly clear by the time of Richard the Lionheart in the twelfth century. Though their prehistoric ancestors did roam in the British Isles, lions as we know them were probably not seen in the capital until the thirteenth century, when records suggest payments were made by King John for the keepers of the lions at the Tower of London. Three lions were given to his son, Henry III, as a wedding gift by the Holy Roman Emperor, Frederick III, and as a result of their royal associations, lions can be seen around the capital in various forms.

Lions of London
ADMIRE THE SOUTH BANK LION

The huge lion which stands on a plinth at the eastern end of Westminster Bridge once surveyed the Thames from the Red Lion Brewery, before it was demolished in 1949 to build the Royal Festival Hall. It also stood briefly outside Waterloo Station.

Designed by William F. Woodington and moulded in Coade stone, an artificial stone created in the Coades' factory in Lambeth, it is also known as the Coade Stone Lion.

Westminster Bridge, SE1
Waterloo tube and railway station

Lions of London
DRINK AT THE RED LION IN CROWN PASSAGE

Reputedly one of London's oldest licensed premises, the Red Lion is a modest little pub with a mixed crowd who drink quietly together without pretension, stirred only by occasional visitors ticking off the Pall Mall square on a Monopoly pub crawl.

Hidden down the tiny alleyway of Crown Passage, a sign declares the Red Lion to be 'London's Last Village Inn'. Legend has it that a tunnel underneath allowed Charles II's mistress Nell Gwyn to access St James's Palace from her home at 79 Pall Mall.

23 Crown Passage, SW1Y 6PP
Green Park tube station

Lions of London
RIDE LANDSEER'S LIONS IN TRAFALGAR SQUARE

Four enormous bronze lions stand at the base of Nelson's Column in Trafalgar Square, created by Victorian painter and sculptor Edwin Landseer after stone versions by Thomas Milnes were deemed inadequate. A painting of Landseer in his studio sculpting a model for the lions is often on show at the National Portrait Gallery, a short walk away.

Visitors who flock to Trafalgar Square often ride on the backs of the beasts, which legend says will spring to life when Big Ben strikes thirteen.

Trafalgar Square, WC2
Charing Cross tube and railway station

Lions of London
FIND THE LION GUARDS OF CHINATOWN

Two Chinese guardian lions stand halfway along Gerrard Street, donated by the People's Republic of China and unveiled in 1985 to mark the 'formal opening' of Soho's Chinatown, despite it having been a centre for the Chinese community since the 1960s.

Lions are a Chinese symbol of protection and power and pairs of lions have guarded entrances to important places in China for centuries, some of the earliest being Han dynasty tombs dating from between 206 BC and 220 AD.

Gerrard Street, W1
Leicester Square tube station

SEE THE ASIATIC LIONS AT LONDON ZOO

Fewer than 400 Asiatic lions remain in the wild worldwide, limited to a single forest in the Indian state of Gujarat, so the small pride at the Zoological Society of London is vital. A number of cubs have been born here.

The lions were once found in a wide area from Greece to India, and are pictured in classical art and literature, but hunting has led them to the brink of extinction. The zoo works with partners in India to try to ensure their survival.

www.zsl.org
Regent's Park, NW1 4RY
Camden Town tube station

HUNT LIONS AT THE BRITISH MUSEUM

The British Museum was protected by a pride of 25 metal lions, on top of railings by Alfred Stevens, removed in 1895, but Sir George Frampton's two stone lions still guard the entrance on Montague Place.

Inside, the 6-ton Lion of Knidos is a highlight of the Great Court. Panels in Room 10a tell of Assyrian lion hunts, and there are lions from the Mausoleum of Halicarnassus in Room 21 and the impressive red granite Prudhoe Lions of Amenhotep III in the Egyptian galleries.

www.britishmuseum.org
Great Russell Street. WC1B 3DG
Tottenham Court Road tube station

WATCH A PLAY AT THE OLD RED LION

There is said to have been a pub on the site of the Old Red Lion in Islington since 1415. It is in the background of William Hogarth's *Evening* and was a favourite haunt of Samuel Johnson and Thomas Paine, who wrote *The Rights of Man* in the courtyard.

It was rebuilt in 1899 and in 1979 the tiny Old Red Lion Theatre opened in the former billiard room. Since then, it has been a centre for experimental theatre and emerging talent.

www.oldredliontheatre.co.uk
418 St John Street, EC1V 4NJ
Angel tube station

Weekend Tips

Allow extra time for the walk from Westminster Bridge past the Houses of Parliament to Trafalgar Square, through Chinatown, and on to the British Museum, where there are scores more lions to be found.

YULETIDE LONDON

London is a special place to spend the Christmas season, with fairy lights, mulled wine, carol concerts, Christmas trees and a festive atmosphere in pubs and shops, as people huddle together to stave off the cold and the dark. The city that inspired *A Christmas Carol* still charms and delights, with frosts and occasional snow flurries, and an unpredictable array of Christmas fairs and events which are announced in late November and bring communities together.

SING CAROLS AT ST MARTIN-IN-THE-FIELDS

As well as being one of central London's most beautiful churches, St Martin-in-the-Fields also does vital work with London's homeless people via a charity Connection at St Martin-in-the-Fields.

Winter can be one of the most difficult times for homeless Londoners, and carol concerts at the church help raise money to ensure that many have a better Christmas. Funds are also drawn from an appeal via BBC Radio 4 which has been broadcast annually since 1924.

www.stmartin-in-the-fields.org
Trafalgar Square, WC2N 4JJ
Charing Cross tube and railway station

SHELTER AND REST AT THE COCK TAVERN

As the Christmas shopping season kicks in, most Londoners will inevitably find themselves on Oxford Street at some point, in need of an escape from the endless crowds. The Cock Tavern, on Great Portland Street, provides one such haven.

A pretty little corner pub built around 1904 by pub architects Bird and Walters, it offers comfortable seating, wood panelling and an open fire, as well as a nice pint of ale to help relieve shopping stress.

27 Great Portland Street, W1W 8QE
Oxford Circus tube station

BAG SEASONAL TREATS AT FORTNUM'S FOOD HALL

Established in 1707 by William Fortnum and Hugh Mason, luxury grocer Fortnum & Mason on Piccadilly is a favourite of the Queen, and has held royal warrants for more than 150 years.

As Christmas Day approaches, Fortnum's attracts shoppers with its elaborate seasonal window displays, and hordes head there to pick up special items to supplement their Christmas dinner, and buy hampers for colleagues and loved ones.

www.fortnumandmason.com
181 Piccadilly, W1A 1ER
Green Park tube station

FIND A CHRISTMAS TREE AT CAMDEN GARDEN CENTRE

Buying a real Christmas tree in central London can be harder than one might imagine, but Camden Garden Centre do a roaring trade each year. Their clients include the London Dungeon, Tower Bridge and 11 Downing Street.

Though buying a real tree is expensive anywhere nowadays, customers can at least rest assured that the centre is owned by the Camden Garden Centre Charitable Trust, founded in 1983 to tackle youth unemployment in the area, and all money raised goes straight back into their projects.

www.camdengardencentre.co.uk
2 Barker Drive, St Pancras Way, NW1 0JW
Camden Road tube and overground station

BUY A WREATH ON COLUMBIA ROAD

For the rest of the year, Columbia Road's Sunday morning flower market is known for colourful and exotic blooms, but in December it switches to greens and reds as seasonal decorations take over. Alongside wreaths, the stalls are full of Christmas trees, holly, mistletoe and scarlet poinsettias.

Established in the 1860s, the market was once held on Saturdays, but changed to Sundays to accommodate the large local Jewish population. Columbia Road also boasts some excellent independent shops, great for picking up unusual gifts.

www.columbiaroad.info
Columbia Road, E2 7RG
Old Street tube and railway station

WINTER 192 THE WEEKENDS START HERE

Weekend Tips

London Walks (www.walks.com) run public walks led by experienced guides all year round, but their Christmas walks on long dark evenings are a particular highlight.

Yuletide London

WALK THROUGH LEADENHALL MARKET

In *A Christmas Carol*, Charles Dickens pictured Ebenezer Scrooge in a town house believed to have been on the site of the Lloyd's of London building behind Leadenhall Market. The market and the streets and alleyways around it still exude a Victorian charm.

Though its shops are quiet on Saturdays and Sundays, the cobbled alleyways are best seen without the crowds in any case, giving space to admire the arches designed in 1881 by Sir Horace Jones.

www.cityoflondon.gov.uk
Gracechurch Street, EC3V 1LR
Monument tube station

Yuletide London

GO ICE SKATING AT THE TOWER OF LONDON

One of many outdoor skating rinks that pop up around the city over the Christmas period, the ice rink at the Tower of London sits neatly beneath the fortress battlements in the hollow of the moat, which was filled in in the 1840s.

The rink offers full skate hire, with sessions extending into the evening to allow floodlit after-dark skating, and even a glass of mulled wine to warm up afterwards.

www.hrp.org.uk
The Tower of London, EC3N 4AB
Tower Hill tube station

FISHERMEN'S LONDON

Though it may not strike visitors as a fishing town, London was once home to one of Britain's largest fishing fleets. Hewlett's Short Blue Fleet sailed out from Barking for weeks at a time, bringing back fresh fish to Billingsgate Fish Market in the City of London, where it was a lifeline for undernourished Londoners. Though that industry is a distant memory, Billingsgate Market still sells fresh fish daily, albeit from a new site in Docklands, and Londoners maintain the same taste for fish that they have always had.

Fishermen's London
BUY FISH AT BILLINGSGATE MARKET

On Saturdays the UK's largest inland fish market begins trading as early as 4 a.m., with crates of live British crabs alongside huge tuna, small sharks and conger eels, and Asian and African fish experts selling exotic produce from around the world.

Billingsgate has been London's fish market since the sixteenth century, when the riverside market at Billingsgate Wharf was the centre of fish trading. In the nineteenth century, it moved to Lower Thames Street, before relocating to Docklands in the 1980s.

www.cityoflondon.gov.uk
Trafalgar Way, Poplar, E14 5ST
Blackwall DLR station

Fishermen's London
SEE THE SAUCY JACK AT VALENCE HOUSE

Barking was once one of Britain's busiest fishing ports, becoming home to a fleet of at least 220 boats by 1850.

With the opening of the railway to Grimsby, Barking's fishing industry began to falter, and when the Great Storm of 1863 killed sixty local fishermen, the fleet transferred to Gorleston. The River Industries Galleries at Dagenham's Valence House Museum tell the history, including a model of local fishing smack the *Saucy Jack*.

www.lbbd.gov.uk
Becontree Avenue, Dagenham, RM8 3HT
Chadwell Heath railway station

Fishermen's London
EAT SEAFOOD AT WILTONS

Wiltons restaurant can trace its history back to 1742, when George William Wilton opened a shellfish stall in the Haymarket, St James's famous street market. It was so successful that by 1805 the family had opened Wiltons Shellfish Mongers and Oyster Rooms in Cockspur Street.

Though the restaurant has moved around, it has never left the safety of St James's, and in 1984 it relocated to its current Jermyn Street home. Owned by the Hambro family since the Second World War, it specialises in excellent seafood for those with deep pockets.

www.wiltons.co.uk
55 Jermyn Street, SW1Y 6LX
Piccadilly Circus tube station

WALK FROM FISHMONGERS' HALL TO OLD BILLINGSGATE

Though the fish trade has moved to the new market in Docklands, historically it was in the heart of the City of London, around the streets where Old Billingsgate Market and Fishmongers' Hall still stand on either side of London Bridge.

Billingsgate began trading in the sixteenth century, but this area has been known for fish for much longer – the hall of the Worshipful Company of Fishmongers has been here since 1434. It is easy to imagine the boats pulling up to the wharf, unloading fish to be inspected by Guildsmen of Fish Hall.

www.fishhall.org.uk
London Bridge, EC4R 9EL
Monument tube station

Fishermen's London
SEE *FISHERMEN CARRYING A DROWNED MAN*

Based on sketches made in the Dutch fishing area of Zandvoort, Jozef Israëls's *Fishermen Carrying a Drowned Man* pictures the body of a fisherman being carried onshore by his companions, against a backdrop of grey sea. The man's wife and children walk in the foreground, overcome by grief.

Though the artist was Dutch, the painting was first exhibited at the Salon in Paris in 1861, before being shown in London at the Royal Academy. It now hangs in Room A at the National Gallery.

www.nationalgallery.org.uk
Room A, The National Gallery, Trafalgar Square, WC2N 5DN
Charing Cross tube and railway station

Weekend Tips

Reward yourself for your very early start at Billingsgate Market and mix with market workers and porters in the cafés for an early morning cuppa and kippers.

Fishermen's London
BROWSE TACKLE AT FARLOWS

Possibly the world's oldest and grandest fishing shop, Farlows was established in the City in 1840 by Charles Farlow. It remained in the family until the last Mrs Farlow retired in 1960.

It specialises in fly fishing, lure fishing and shooting, and provides all the associated equipment such as tweeds, deerstalkers and waders, as you might expect from the shop where Prince Charles gets kitted out for trips to Scotland.

www.farlows.co.uk
9 Pall Mall, SW1Y 5NP
Piccadilly Circus tube station

Fishermen's London
EAT AT LONDON'S OLDEST FISH-AND-CHIP SHOP

Established in 1871, the Rock & Sole Plaice is London's oldest fish-and-chip shop, serving generous portions to Covent Garden locals and visitors using the same 140-year-old recipe.

The premises at 47 Endell Street claims to have been only the third ever fish shop to open its doors, at that time serving workers from Covent Garden market and local factories. Today, the small shop prides itself on using sustainable British fish, with two floors of indoor seating and pleasant pavement tables.

www.rockandsoleplaice.com
47 Endell St, WC2H 9AJ
Tottenham Court Road tube station

MUSICAL LONDON

It was the Swinging Sixties that thrust London's music scene into the global consciousness, with London-based bands like The Beatles, The Rolling Stones, The Kinks and The Who becoming global superstars. However, London's classical music pedigree extends back much further. Baroque composer George Frideric Handel made London his home in 1712, and later a Victorian classical renaissance saw the opening of the Royal Opera House in 1858 and the Royal Albert Hall in 1878. However, London is also known for its ability to attract – and make global stars of – overseas artists such as Jimi Hendrix and Bob Marley.

Musical London
CROSS THE ZEBRA CROSSING AT ABBEY ROAD

The cover of The Beatles' eleventh studio album featured the band on a zebra crossing outside the studios on Abbey Road where it was recorded, and from which it took its name. It went on to become one of the best-selling records of all time.

Beatles pilgrims still flock to recreate the poses of the Fab Four snapped by photographer Iain Macmillan at around 11.30 a.m. on 8 August 1969.

www.abbeyroad.com
Outside 3 Abbey Road, NW8 9AY
St John's Wood tube station

Musical London
SEE A LUNCHTIME CONCERT AT WIGMORE HALL

Celebrated for its near-perfect acoustics, which attract some of the greatest artists of the classical world, Wigmore Hall is a chamber music concert venue best known for its piano, song and instrumental recitals. It hosts more than 400 events each season, including popular lunchtime concerts.

Purpose built in 1901 beside the showrooms of German firm Bechstein whose pianos it showcased, Wigmore Hall was originally known as Bechstein Hall.

www.wigmore-hall.org.uk
36 Wigmore Street, W1U 2BP
Bond Street tube station

Musical London
VISIT HANDEL'S HOUSE

A small independent museum located within the former home of baroque composer George Frideric Handel, Handel House is the best place to get a sense of the man behind the music, and understand what his life in Georgian London might have been like.

Handel lived at 25 Brook Street from 1723 until his death in 1759, composing most of his great works in the half-light of his composition room, before playing them in the rehearsal room which still occasionally hosts recitals today.

www.handelhouse.org
25 Brook Street, Mayfair, W1K 4HB
Bond Street tube station

Musical London
SHOP IN LONDON'S MUSICAL STREET

A must-visit location for those searching for musical instruments in the West End, Denmark Street has been synonymous with British music since the 1950s, as home to music publishers Regent Sounds Studio, where The Who, The Rolling Stones and Black Sabbath have all recorded.

Regent Sounds is now a guitar shop, and shares the street with other musical instrument retailers such as Chris Bryant's Musical Instruments, Denmark Street Guitars, Hanks, Macari's and Wunjo Guitars.

Denmark Street, WC2H
Tottenham Court Road tube station

WATCH A BAND AT THE 100 CLUB

Number 100 Oxford Street began as a music venue in the 1940s. It became Feldman Swing Club, and grew into the London Jazz Club, epicentre of post-war jazz.

By the 1960s, it had become the 100 Club, drawing international names such as Muddy Waters, Bo Diddley and B. B. King, and later punks, including The Sex Pistols, The Clash and the Buzzcocks. Despite occasional threat of closure, it remains at the heart of London music.

www.the100club.co.uk
100 Oxford Street, W1D 1LL
Tottenham Court Road tube station

LEARN ABOUT INSTRUMENTS AT THE HORNIMAN

Though many associate it with stuffed animals and anthropology, Forest Hill's Horniman Museum is home to a nationally designated collection of musical instruments, with more than 1,300 on display in the Music Gallery, including some from the V&A collection.

Alongside those in display cases, the Horniman offers the chance to make music using some interesting and unusual instruments in a side gallery, and boasts an outdoor sound garden with large instruments for everyone to play.

www.horniman.ac.uk
100 London Road, Forest Hill, SE23 3PQ
Forest Hill overground station

VISIT A LONDON POP VIDEO LOCATION

Though music videos were not big business until the 1980s, earlier promotional videos were shot in London. Bob Dylan's flashcards for 'Subterranean Homesick Blues' were filmed on Savoy Steps, and The Beatles' final gig performed on top of 3 Savile Row was cut into five videos.

For fans of 1990s pop, the Spice Girls' 'Wannabee' was filmed in the St Pancras Hotel, The Prodigy's 'Firestarter' in the disused Aldwych tube station and The Verve's 'Bittersweet Symphony' in Hoxton Street.

Savoy Steps, WC2R 0AA and elsewhere
Embankment tube station

Weekend Tips

Not far from Wigmore Hall and Handel's House, there are good restaurants in St Christopher's Place (Marylebone, London W1U).

SCIENTIFIC LONDON

Since the beginning of the eighteenth century, London has been a capital of science – birthplace of Michael Faraday, Rosalind Franklin and Tim Berners-Lee, and home to scientific greats Sir Isaac Newton, Sir Humphry Davy and Charles Darwin. It is the city in which penicillin was discovered, in the Paddington laboratory of Sir Alexander Fleming, and television was invented in John Logie Baird's upstairs workshop in Frith Street, Soho. It remains at the forefront of scientific thought, with research and teaching at Imperial College and University College London rated amongst the best in the world.

VISIT THE SCIENCE MUSEUM

With a collection of over 300,000 items that brings together Stephenson's Rocket, the Apollo 10 command module, a Model T Ford and the first jet engine, the Science Museum in South Kensington provides a whistle-stop tour through the history of science over seven floors.

Founded in 1857 and made independent in 1909, the museum attracts more than 2 million visitors a year, with ever-changing galleries reacting to the latest scientific discoveries.

www.sciencemuseum.org.uk
Exhibition Road, South Kensington, SW7 2DD
South Kensington tube station

SEE THE BROAD STREET PUMP

In the summer of 1854, Soho was gripped with cholera, which many assumed was caused by air pollution. Having tested the water and mapped cases clustered in the surrounding streets, Dr John Snow traced the source to water drawn from a pump on Broad Street. Local authorities were persuaded to remove the handle.

The spot is marked with a pink paving slab outside the John Snow pub on what is now Broadwick Street, and a replica pump stands nearby.

www.johnsnowsociety.org
39 Broadwick Street, Soho, W1F 9QJ
Oxford Circus tube station

ATTEND A LECTURE AT THE ROYAL SOCIETY

Officially called the Royal Society of London for the Improvement of Natural Knowledge, the Royal Society in Carlton House Terrace, founded in the 1660s, is the oldest scientific society. It is still a meeting place for the world's most eminent scientists, just as it was when Sir Christopher Wren and Sir Isaac Newton were members.

The Royal Society runs a series of free public events and lectures, covering a range of topics in the world of science, scientific history, technology, engineering, medicine and mathematics.

www.royalsociety.org
6–9 Carlton House Terrace, SW1Y 5AG
Charing Cross tube and railway station

DRINK AT THE DEVEREUX

The late seventeenth century was the age of the coffee house, and members of the Royal Society and other great men of learning gathered informally at the Grecian Coffee House in Devereux Court to discuss the issues of the day.

After watching the dissection of a dolphin that swum up the Thames, it was here that Sir Isaac Newton, astronomer Edmond Halley and Sir Hans Sloane retired to consider it. Though the original coffee house has long gone, the pub has taken its place.

20 Devereux Court, Temple, WC2R 3JJ
Temple tube station

Scientific London
VISIT THE HOME OF TIME

The Royal Observatory at Greenwich has been the centre of world time since the International Meridian Conference of 1884.

The original observatory was built for the Astronomer Royal, John Flamsteed, and still carries his name, Flamsteed House. Displays chart the history of astronomical and navigational equipment and allow access to the Astronomer Royal's apartments and the Octagon Room, where Flamsteed made his observations.

www.rmg.co.uk
Blackheath Avenue, SE10 8XJ
Cutty Sark for Maritime Greenwich DLR station

Scientific London
CLIMB THE EXPERIMENTAL LIGHTHOUSE

With no jagged rocks or rolling waves, the presence of the Experimental Lighthouse at Trinity Buoy Wharf is something of a surprise. Built in 1864 to develop lighting techniques for Trinity House's lighthouses and lightships, it was one of a pair of lighthouses on the banks of the Thames.

Michael Faraday worked on some of the earliest electric lighthouse lighting here, and today it is home to Longplayer, a 1,000-year-long musical composition set to run until the final seconds of the year 2999.

www.longplayer.org
Trinity Buoy Wharf, 64 Orchard Place, E14 0JY
East India DLR station

Scientific London
EXPLORE THE WELLCOME COLLECTION

The Wellcome Trust is a medical charity established in 1936 in the will of pharmaceutical magnate Sir Henry Wellcome, who left his collection and an endowment now worth £14.5 billion in order to further medical science.

The collection opened in 2007, displaying a series of permanent and changing exhibitions with a wide-ranging brief to explore ideas about the connections between medicine, life and art. It also features a café and bookshop.

www.wellcomecollection.org
183 Euston Road, NW1 2BE
Euston Square tube station

Weekend Tips

For a change of perspective, a combination of the number 129 bus and the Emirates Airline is a fine way to get from Greenwich to Trinity Buoy Wharf.

ANCIENT LONDON

Though many assume that London began with the Romans in AD 50, legends drawn from the *Historia Brittonum* suggest it was founded by Brutus of Troy in 1070 BC. The truth is unclear, but people certainly lived in London before the Romans, as burial mounds, earthworks and neolithic axes are common. London's rich natural history also pre-dates the Romans by many thousands of years, and hippopotamus and elephant remains have been found under Trafalgar Square, along with a mammoth on the Strand and a rhinoceros beneath Battersea Power Station.

DISCOVER THE SITE OF THE ICENI'S LAST STAND

An Iron Age hill fort in what is now the Epping Forest, Ambresbury Banks is an enclosed area of 9 acres, surrounded by ancient banks of earth originally 3 metres high, and protected by 3-metre ditches built by local people in 500 BC.

According to legend, Ambresbury Banks was the site of the defeat and death of the great Queen Boudicca of the Iceni, killed in battle against the Romans in AD 61. Though the site of her death is disputed, this wooded site evokes the ancient landscapes of Britain.

www.cityoflondon.gov.uk
Ambresbury Banks, Epping Forest, Essex, CM16 5HN
Theydon Bois tube station

SEEK OUT CAESAR'S WELL

The source of the River Ravensbourne at Keston, in London's far south-east, is a spring and holy well which legend has it provided Caesar's army with water. Thirsty soldiers, who camped here in 55 BC, followed a raven to the hidden spring.

Today the well, a circular brick basin in a wooded glade, still feeds the ponds of Keston Common. Earthworks of what is known as Caesar's Camp also remain visible nearby, though these are actually part of a much earlier Iron Age hill fort.

Westerham Road, Keston, Bromley, BR2
Hayes railway station

VISIT ST PANCRAS OLD CHURCH

St Pancras Old Church was rebuilt in 1847 on a site that is believed to have been home to a Christian church since at least 314 AD, one of the oldest places of Christian worship in England.

The Victorian replacement contains parts of the older church, with Roman bricks and Norman masonry in the north wall of the nave. The tomb of Sir John Soane lies in the graveyard, along with those of composer Johann Christian Bach and sculptor John Flaxman.

www.posp.co.uk
Pancras Road, NW1 1UL
King's Cross St Pancras tube and railway stations

SEARCH FOR QUEEN BOUDICCA'S GRAVE

One poetic legend suggests that after the defeat of the Iceni by the Romans, Queen Boudicca's remains were carried up onto what is now Hampstead Heath.

A counter-claim suggests the Queen's remains lie beneath platform 10 of King's Cross station, and it seems unlikely that her final resting place will ever be discovered. Nevertheless, folklore still continues to name the tumulus on the northern slopes of Parliament Hill 'Boudicca's Mound'.

www.cityoflondon.gov.uk
Parliament Hill Fields, Hampstead Heath, NW5
Hampstead Heath overground station

Ancient London
STAND BESIDE A 2,000-YEAR-OLD YEW

Probably London's oldest living thing, the Totteridge Yew stands in the graveyard of St Andrew's in Totteridge, just as it has for up to 2,000 years. It measures 8 metres (25 feet) in circumference, little changed from the earliest records made in the seventeenth century.

The tree has been a focal point for countless generations. It is said that primitive court hearings took place in its shadow, and a baby found abandoned by it in 1722 was named Henry Totteridge.

www.totteridgechurch.org.uk
St Andrew's Parish Church, Totteridge, N20 8PR
Totteridge & Whetstone tube station

Ancient London
SEE A ROMAN MOSAIC IN SOUTHWARK CATHEDRAL

At Southwark Cathedral, which is close to the Roman highway of Watling Street, a section of Roman mosaic was found in the floor of the south choir aisle in the nineteenth century.

A collection of Roman sculptures was also discovered in a well beneath the choir in 1977, now displayed beside the archaeological chamber in the Lancelot's Link passageway. All these suggest that this may have also been a site of Roman worship.

www.cathedral.southwark.anglican.org
London Bridge, SE1 9DA
London Bridge tube and railway station

Weekend Tips

The Orange Tree pub (Totteridge Village, N20 8NX) is across the road from the Totteridge Yew, and Southwark Cathedral has a good refectory (London Bridge, SE1 9DA).

Ancient London
LOOK FOR PREHISTORIC MAN IN VAUXHALL

They may not look much, but the wooden posts which can be seen dotting the Thames foreshore in front of Vauxhall's MI6 building at low tide are the oldest structures ever to have been found in London.

The timbers were originally built on dry land, near where the River Effra enters the Thames. Mesolithic stone tools found nearby are thought to be the remains of a prehistoric structure, constructed using trees felled between 4790 and 4490 BC.

www.thamesdiscovery.org
Thames foreshore, Vauxhall, SW8
Vauxhall tube and railway station

GEORGIAN LONDON

The Georgian period was a time of great change in
London. As it began in 1714, the Act of Union had just
been signed, the City had only recently been rebuilt after
the Great Fire and London had a population of less than
700,000. By 1830, the capital had been transformed –
there were more than twice as many people, new styles of
architecture were taking over, the Industrial Revolution
was under way and Londoners were drinking tea, playing
sports, reading newspapers and wearing new fashions.
Understanding Georgian London helps understand
the city we see today.

Georgian London
TAKE A TOUR OF SOMERSET HOUSE

Sir William Chambers's spectacular neoclassical palace by the Thames was completed in 1776, and still has the power to impress most who enter its grand central courtyard. Regular tours of the site take place on Saturdays, with tickets available from the desk in Seamen's Hall.

Originally designed as a replacement for various government buildings hidden away in back streets, today Somerset House retains a public role, with the Courtauld Institute of Art in the north wing, and public galleries in the south.

www.somersethouse.org.uk
The Strand, WC2R 1LA
Temple tube station

Georgian London
WANDER IN BEDFORD SQUARE

One of the best-preserved Georgian squares in London, Bloomsbury's Bedford Square was constructed between 1776 and 1780, probably designed by the architect Thomas Leverton. Blue plaques identify the former homes of Indian scholar Ram Mohan Roy, Lord Chancellor Lord Eldon and scientist Henry Cavendish.

The square was largely unscathed by the bombs of the Blitz, and though most of the houses are now offices, many for academic institutions, it still appears much the same as when first constructed.

Bedford Square, WC1B
Tottenham Court Road tube station

Georgian London
DINE AT THE WALLACE COLLECTION

There can be few London eateries with as grand a setting as the Wallace Restaurant, set among the trees in the grand glass atrium and sculpture garden at Hertford House, constructed in 1776.

Since 1900, the house has been home to the Wallace Collection, Sir Richard Wallace's unrivalled collection of eighteenth-century art and furniture. The restaurant is open daily, with extended hours on Friday and Saturday evenings offering the chance to dine under the stars.

www.wallacecollection.org
Hertford House, Manchester Square, W1U 3BN
Bond Street tube station

Georgian London
SURVEY THE HORSES OF HORSE GUARDS

At the head of Horse Guards Parade, where the monarch traditionally inspects the troops in Trooping the Colour, the Horse Guards building designed by John Vardy and William Kent was completed in 1753, during the reign of George II.

Horse Guards is the official entrance to St James's Palace and Buckingham Palace, and is guarded by the Queen's Life Guard, some on horseback, others standing. The Changing of the Guard takes place daily at 11 a.m., or 10 a.m. on Sundays.

www.royal.gov.uk
Horse Guards, Whitehall, SW1A 2AX
Westminster tube station

Georgian London

VISIT ST GEORGE'S BLOOMSBURY

The sixth and last church commissioned from Nicholas Hawksmoor as part of the Commission for Building Fifty New Churches, St George's Bloomsbury was consecrated in 1730. It is open to the public daily from 1 to 4 p.m.

It features a distinctive stepped tower, based on a Roman description of the mausoleum at Halicarnassus, and topped by a statue of George I in Roman dress. The grand portico is based on the Temple of Bacchus in Lebanon.

www.stgeorgesbloomsbury.org.uk
Bloomsbury Way, WC1A 2SR
Holborn tube station

Georgian London

SEE WELLINGTON'S BOOTS AT APSLEY HOUSE

Standing proudly on Hyde Park Corner, at an address famously known as 'Number 1 London', Apsley House was acquired by the Duke of Wellington in 1817, and extended under the supervision of architect Benjamin Dean Wyatt to become his London home.

The grand house is open to the public as a museum of the first Duke's life and work, as well as his art collection, and deep in the basement a display case features a pair of his famous boots.

www.english-heritage.org.uk
149 Piccadilly, Hyde Park Corner, W1J 7NT
Hyde Park Corner tube station

Georgian London

LEARN DOMESTIC HISTORY AT THE GEFFRYE MUSEUM

Hackney's Geffrye Museum is situated within a set of Georgian almshouses. Though they no longer provide for pensioners, they are largely intact and have been a museum since 1914, recreating historic English domestic interiors.

One of the almshouses, Number 14, is also occasionally opened to demonstrate what life would have been like here for the pensioners of the eighteenth and nineteenth centuries.

www.geffrye-museum.org.uk
136 Kingsland Road, E2 8EA
Hoxton overground station

Weekend Tips

The Geffrye Museum can be accessed by the 55 bus from Oxford Street, and has a good licensed café, serving tea, cake and main meals during museum opening hours.

CIRCUS LONDON

Though court jesters have been around much longer, the modern circus is often dated to 9 January 1768, when Sergeant Major Philip Astley first performed on horseback near Waterloo. He created Astley's Amphitheatre of Equestrian Arts, joined by strongman Signor Colpi and clowns Fortunelly and Burt. By the mid-nineteenth century there were hundreds of circuses operating in Britain, and London continues to celebrate its rich culture and history of circus arts.

ATTEND THE CLOWNS' CHURCH SERVICE

Every year on the first Sunday in February, the clowning great and good gather at a church in Dalston for the Clowns' service of remembrance, dedicated to father of modern clowning Joseph Grimaldi.

Held in St James's Chapel on Pentonville Road, where Grimaldi was buried, until it was closed in the 1950s, the service later moved to Holy Trinity in Dalston. A candle is lit for every clown who has died during the previous year.

www.clowns-international.com
Beechwood Road, Dalston, Hackney, E8 3DY
Dalston Junction overground station

LEARN WITH THE NATIONAL CENTRE FOR CIRCUS ARTS

Established in 1989 as Circus Space, the National Centre for Circus Arts is housed in the old Shoreditch Electric Light Station in Hoxton, and uses the huge space to educate students in acrobatics and cirque nouveau skills.

As well as offering a degree in Circus Arts, the centre welcomes amateurs to test their nerve with circus experience days and introductions to skills like trapeze, tightrope, juggling and acrobatics.

www.nationalcircus.org.uk
Coronet Street, N1 6HD
Old Street tube and railway station

CATCH A SHOW AT ZIPPOS CIRCUS

One of the last remaining travelling circuses, Zippos is owned by Martin Burton, aka Zippo the Clown, and has been touring for over twenty-five years. The tour begins each year as early as February in London, before moving around the country.

Zippos remains popular with the crowds, and has received official recognition with ringmaster Norman Barrett being awarded an MBE in 2010 for more than sixty years' service in the ring.

www.zipposcircus.co.uk

GET JUGGLING AT ODDBALLS

During the mid-1980s, performer Phillip Maxwell-Stewart, also known by his stage name Max Oddball, set up Oddballs, a one-stop shop for all juggling paraphernalia.

England's 'original juggling shop' is found in Camden Lock Market. Balls, sticks, clubs, diabolos and unicycles are just some of the kit on sale, and trained jugglers are on hand to offer advice.

www.oddballs.co.uk
200a–b Camden Lock Place, Chalk Farm Road, NW1 8AB
Camden Town tube station

Circus London
TAKE A WALK IN JOSEPH GRIMALDI PARK

A park dedicated to the father of modern clowning is found in Islington. Joseph Grimaldi Park commemorates the man born in London in 1778, son of an Italian father who met his mother when they both worked at the Drury Lane Theatre.

The park was once home to the Pentonville Chapel, demolished in the 1980s, and Grimaldi was buried in the graveyard, where his memorial can still be found.

Pentonville Road, N1
King's Cross St Pancras tube and railway stations

Circus London
WATCH STREET CIRCUS IN COVENT GARDEN

Street performers have been present in Covent Garden since the seventeenth century, when Samuel Pepys recalls watching an Italian puppet show. Today the acts, seen and heard in the North Hall, West Piazza and Courtyard, are better than ever.

The standard is so high that the market holds auditions for the chance to perform in its most prized pitches, competing with the great theatres in surrounding streets.

www.coventgardenlondonuk.com
The Market, Covent Garden, WC2
Covent Garden tube station

Circus London
FIND WOMBWELL'S TOMB

Prior to the opening of London Zoo, England afforded few opportunities to see exotic beasts in the flesh, until Essex boy George Wombwell founded Wombwell's Travelling Menagerie in 1810.

He began his zoological life showing snakes in London pubs, and eventually had the largest travelling menagerie in England, whose animals were shown three times before Prince Albert and Queen Victoria. His lion Nero sleeps atop his grave in Highgate West Cemetery.

www.highgatecemetery.org
Highgate Cemetery, Swain's Lane, N6 6PJ
Archway tube station

Weekend Tips

The Flask in Highgate (77 Highgate West Hill, Camden, N6 6BU) is a great pub, just up the hill from the cemetery.

BIBLIOPHILES' LONDON

London has had a huge influence on world literature, with London writers such as William Shakespeare and Charles Dickens dominating English-language writing. Perhaps by virtue of their literary heritage, Londoners have always been avid readers, and the bookshops here are among the best in the world. London continues to be a city of writers, so browsing for paperbacks offers the possibility of the next person through the bookshop door being a future Nobel Laureate or Man Booker Prize winner.

VISIT LIMEHOUSE FOR LITERARY INSPIRATION

The area of Limehouse, a significant port since late medieval times, has inspired generations of writers. Oscar Wilde featured it in *The Picture of Dorian Gray*, and in *The Man with the Twisted Lip* Sherlock Holmes visited local opium dens in search of clues.

Charles Dickens's godfather Christopher Huffam ran his chandlery business here, and local pub The Grapes appears in the opening chapter of *Our Mutual Friend*. It retains a complete works of Dickens for the use of patrons.

www.thegrapes.co.uk
76 Narrow Street, London E14 8BP
Westferry DLR station

EXAMINE THE TREASURES OF THE BRITISH LIBRARY

The British Library receives a copy of every publication produced in the UK and Ireland, and its collection extends to over 150 million items.

Some of the library's greatest treasures are exhibited in the Sir John Ritblat Gallery, with changing displays of items ranging from Magna Carta to religious texts such as the Gutenberg Bible, notebooks from Leonardo da Vinci, letters from Henry VIII and even handwritten lyrics from The Beatles.

www.bl.uk
96 Euston Road, NW1 2DB
King's Cross St Pancras tube and railway stations

EXPLORE LITERARY BLOOMSBURY

A plaque at 50 Gordon Square commemorates the Bloomsbury Group of writers and intellectuals, and Virginia Woolf lived at number 46, with siblings Adrian and Vanessa. Charles Dickens lived at 48 Doughty Street.

Nearby, 21 Russell Square is where Oscar Wilde spent his final evening in London, T. S. Eliot worked at 24 Russell Square as an editor for Faber & Faber and the British Museum's Reading Room was used by Mark Twain, Bram Stoker, George Bernard Shaw, Rudyard Kipling, H. G. Wells and George Orwell.

Bloomsbury, WC1
Russell Square tube station

BUY BOOKS AT SKOOB

Occupying a vast subterranean lair beneath Bloomsbury's Brunswick Centre, Skoob has been one of London's leading second-hand bookshops for over thirty years.

Established in 1979, Skoob claims to have a million books lurking in a warehouse in Oxfordshire, from which they draw their 55,000 shop stock. It is popular with students from the nearby University of London, not least because the owners promise that the books cost at most half of their equivalent new price.

www.skoob.com
Unit 66, The Brunswick Shopping Centre, Marchmont Street, WC1N 1AE
Russell Square tube station

EAT CAKE AT THE *LONDON REVIEW* CAKE SHOP

A modern twist on London's literary coffee houses, the *London Review* Cake Shop holds events, discussions, talks and debates, and stays opens until 6.30 p.m. to allow for early-evening reading over tea and cake.

It was opened in 2007 by the *London Review of Books*, an addition to a shop opened in 2003 which now boasts 20,000 titles. Both combine to make a great destination for bookish types in need of intellectual stimulus and physical nourishment.

www.londonreviewbookshop.co.uk
14 Bury Place, WC1A 2JL
Holborn tube station

GO TO THE SHERLOCK HOLMES MUSEUM

The world's most famous fictional detective lived at 221b Baker Street, and his imaginary home has been maintained as a museum to him since 1990. Visitors are transported into the world inhabited by the famous detective, with waxworks, labelled artefacts and items relevant to the books.

The listed building features a mock-up of Holmes's apartment, with his rooms and those of Dr Watson as well as a laboratory and bathroom, all fitted out with period furnishings.

www.sherlock-holmes.co.uk
221b Baker Street, NW1 6XE
Baker Street tube station

BROWSE AT ANY AMOUNT OF BOOKS

Though its shop on Charing Cross Road may seem small, Any Amount of Books stuffs thousands of books onto its dusty shelves, with rare and antiquarian tomes and first editions as likely to be on sale as bargain paperbacks.

The shop itself has been trading books since at least the 1920s, when it was owned by A. H. Mayhew, a publisher of books on folklore. The owners are willing to travel around the world in search of rare collections.

www.anyamountofbooks.com
56 Charing Cross Road, WC2H 0QA
Leicester Square tube station

Weekend Tips

Bloomsbury's Marchmont Street is known for its independent restaurants, pubs and shops, including the School of Life at number 70, home of philosophical books and courses, and The Marquis Cornwallis pub at number 31.

INDEX BY LOCATION

CENTRAL

All Hallows by the Tower 179
Anrep Mosaics (National Gallery) 60
Any Amount of Books 217
Bedford Square 207
Benjamin Franklin House 32
Bloomsbury 216
Bloomsbury Lanes 33
Café in the Crypt 178
Canaletto's works 143
Cartoon Museum 160
Charles Dickens Museum 174
Church of St Mary Aldermanbury,
   remains of 75
Cork and Bottle 179
Covent Garden street performers 214
Denmark Street 198
Deveraux pub 201
Easter Island Moai (British Museum) 30
Fishermen Carrying a Drowned Man
   (Israëls) 196
43 Cloth Fair 37
Frightfest 115
Golden Jubilee Bridges 155
Hadrian's bust (British Museum) 144
Hogarth's *Election* 159
Hoxne Hoard (British Museum) 47
Impressionists (Courtauld Gallery) 51
Japanese Galleries 94
Japanese roof garden (School of Oriental
   and African Studies) 42
Jewellery Quarter 47
jewellery quarter 47
Joe Allen 33
L. Cornelissen & Son 18
Lamb 175
lions at British Museum 187

London Review Cake Shop 217
London Silver Vaults 48
London's mini Korea 127
London's musical street 198
London's oldest fish-and-chip shop 196
Mon Plaisir 51
Mond Crucifixion (Raphael) 30
National Gallery 19, 30, 60, 143, 196
National Portrait Gallery 160
Old Curiosity Shop 174
Poetry Café 56
Poets' Church (St Giles-in-the-Fields) 57
pop video locations 199
Pushkin House 59
Rock & Sole Plaice 196
St Clement Danes 60
St George's, Bloomsbury 210
St Martin-in-the-Fields carols 189
St Martin-in-the-Fields crypt 178
St Paul's, Covent Garden 45
St Peter's (Italian) Church 145
Seti I, sarcophagus of 178
Simpson's-in-the-Strand 175
Sir John Soane's Museum 159, 178
Skoob 216
Somerset House 51, 207
Swedenborg bookshop 172
Tea House (Covent Garden) 95
Trafalgar Square lions 186
Treasure of Seven Dials 47

NORTH

Abbey Road zebra crossing 198
Alexandra Palace 166
Asiatic lions, London Zoo 187
Boudicca's grave 204
British Library 216
Buttery Café, Burgh House 124
Camden Garden Centre 190
Canons Park 106
Circus Space 212
Daiwa Foundation 41
Dollis Valley Greenwalk 71
East and West Lodges, Euston
   station 37

Emirates Stadium 132
Estorick Collection 145
Fairlop Waters 103
Fenton House 122
Flask, Hampstead 167
Foxburrows Farm 103
Freemasons Arms skittle alley 123
Goldfinger's house 122
Harrow churchyard 38
Highgate Village and Wood 166
Hill Garden and Pergola 123
Jacksons Lane 166
Japan House 41
Jelling Stone 172
Jewish Museum 129
Joseph Grimaldi Park 214
Keats's Garden 57
Kenwood House 123
London Irish Centre 129
London Zoo, Asiatic lions at 187
Lost City of Watling Street 48
Lower Terrace, Hampstead 122
Marx's grave 141
Metroland 37
Odballs 213
Old St Andrew's Church 148
1 Devonshire Terrace 175
Parliament Hill 167
St Pancras Old Church 204
St Pancras station 37
Sherlock Holmes museum 217
Shri Sanatan Hindu Mandir 127
Stables Gallery and Art Centre 106
Swiss Cottage 106
Totteridge Yew 205
221b Baker Street 217
Waterlow Park 167
Wellcome Collection 202
Welsh Harp Open Space 148
Wombwell's tomb 214

EAST

Ambresbury Banks 204
Aquatics Centre 132
ArcelorMittal Orbit 154

Beale Arboretum 23
Beefeaters at Tower of London 98
Billingsgate Market 194
Bloody Tower 100
Bow Creek Ecology Park 108
Brick Lane street art 18
Broadway Market 182
Butterworth Distribution Ceremony 29
Ceremony of the Keys 99
clowns' church service 212
Columbia Road flowermarket 192
Experimental Lighthouse 202
Geffrye Museum 210
Great Eastern slipway 152
Gunpowder Park 84
Hackney City Farm 181
Hackney Empire 184
Hackney Marshes 84, 115
Hackney Museum 184
Hackney's oldest house 181
Hollow Ponds 86
Huguenot Spitalfields 51
ice skating at Tower of London 192
Iceni's last stand 204
Ingrebourne Valley and Hill 104
Island Gardens 119
Leadenhall Market 192
Lee Valley Velopark 82
Lenin's London 140
Limehouse 216
Line of Kings 98
London Fields Lido 181
Miller's House 81
Mudchute City Farm 86
19 Princelet Street 127
Northern Outfall Sewer 150
Old Billingsgate Market and
   Fishmongers' Hall 195
Olympic Park 81
Pages of Hackney 184
Pillboxes of Hornchurch Park 75
Pride of Spitalfields 135
Purfleet Heritage and Military Centre
   104
Queen Elizabeth's Hunting Lodge 26
Royal Beasts 98

Sailortown 119
St Bartholomew the Great 29
St Paul's Cathedral 29
Shard 99
Shoreditch street art 18
Spa Fields 140
Spitalfields City Farm 29
Stratford East 108
street art 18
Sutton House tea room 181
Thames, canoeing on 154
Theatre Royal, Stratford East 108
Tobacco Dock 120
Tower Bridge 99
Tower of London 98–100
Trent Country Park 23
Trinity Buoy Wharf 81, 202
Truman Brewery 136
Upminster Windmill and Tithe Barn 103
Wapping pirate pubs 119
West Lodge Park Hotel 23
White Tower 98
Whitechapel Bell Foundry 34
Wick Woodland 84
Widow's Buns Ceremony 29
William Morris Gallery 25
Wilton's Music Hall 38

SOUTH

Abbey Wood Caravan Club Site 22
Abraham Lincoln: The Man 32
Addington Hills 14
Beckenham Place 111
Belgrave Square statues 139
Bonnington Square Gardens 87
Boot and Flogger 163
Boston Manor House 147
Brockwell and Ladywell Cemeteries 70
Brompton Oratory 59
Burgess Park, barbecue areas in 113
Caesar's well and camp 204
Champion Hill Stadium 131
Charlton House Gardens 110
Charlton Lido 110
Chelsea Physic Garden 94

Churchill War Rooms 74
Clore Gallery 19
Crofton Royal Villa, Orpington 78
Cross Farthing Downs 16
Crossness Pumping Station 151
Cutty Sark 96
Danson Park 77
Darwin's Thinking Walk 79
De Gaulle, Charles (statue) 50
dinosaur hunting, Crystal Palace Park
   111
Embankment 23
Emirates Air Line 156
England's oldest art gallery (Dulwich) 19
Faesten Dic Trail 78
Fan Museum 95
Farlows fishing shop 196
Ferryman's Seat 162
Finnish church 171
575 Wandsworth Road 129
Foots Cray Meadows 78
Foxley Wood 16
Gabriel's Wharf 163
Geraldine Mary Harmsworth Park 22
Godstone Vineyard 134
Golden Hinde II 120
Great Vine 67
Greenland Dock 171
Greenwich Foot Tunnel 179
Greenwich Park 22, 86
Greenwich Park deer 71
Hall Place and Gardens 78
Happy Valley 16
Hayward Gallery 164
High Elms Country Park 79
Holy Trinity, Sloan Square 26
Horniman Museum 199
Horse Guards Parade (Trooping of the
   Colour) 51, 208
Houses of Parliament 159
Ice Age Trees 22
Imperial War Museum 73
John Smith House 159
Kensington Crêperie 51
Kings Arms 113
Kobe earthquake (Natural History

Museum) 41
Konditor & Cook 95
La Médiathèque 52
Labour's former HQ 159
Latin liberators, statues of 139
Leake Street Tunnel 178
Lesnes Abbey Woods 69
London's deepest platform (Hampstead)
   177
London's oldest structure 205
Marshalsea Prison 174
Masters Super Fish 108
Merton Abbey Mills 25
Mitcham Cricket Green 132
Morden Park 131
Mottingham Tarn 110
Museum of Garden History 44
Nunhead Hill 155
O'Higgins, Bernardo, statue of 139
Oxleas Wood Café 110
Oxo Tower 155
Palace of Westminster 159
Pankhurst, Emmeline, statue of 140
Parliament Square 32
pelicans in St James's Park 107
Peter the Great statue (Deptford) 61
Pickering Place 32
Pissarro's inspiration 19
Poets' Corner 56
Polish Hearth Club 59
Prestat 30
Princes Arcade 30
Queen's Orchard 22
RAF Bomber Command 73
Red House Garden 25
Red Lion (Crown Passage) 186
Red Lion (Westminster) 159
Riddlesdown's trackways 13
River Quaggy, Chinbrook Meadows 111
Roman mosaic in Southwark Cathedral
   205
Rose Playhouse 162
Royal Observatory 202
Royal Society 201
Ruskin Park 86
Saison Poetry Library 56

Saucy Jack 194
Saviour's Dock cross 174
Saxon Kings' Stone 65
Science Museum 201
77a Westow Hill 19
Skull and Crossbones, original 119
South Bank lion 186
South London Gallery 18
South Norwood Country Park 13
Southbank Mosaics (St John's
   churchyard) 45
Syon Park 147
Tamesis Dock 164
Tate Britain 20
Thames Barrier 152
Thames, boating on 92
Thames, speedboat on 113
Trooping of the Colour 51, 87, 208
Twickenham, home of rugby 131
V&A Museum 27, 47, 94
V&S Jewellery Gallery 47
Victoria & Albert Refreshment Room 27
Vinopolis 135
Westminster Bridge 55
White Bear, Fickleshole 13
Wiltons Shellfish Mongers 194
Wimbledon Lawn Tennis Museum 131
Winchester Palace Rose Window 162
Windrush Square 128
Zaibatsu Japanese restaurant 42

WEST

Apsley House 210
Bar Italia 143
Battle of Britain Bunker 73
Bedford Park 38
Brent Lodge Park 148
Broad Street Pump 201
Chinatown, lion guards of 186
Coach and Horses 134
Cock Tavern 189
Drayton Court Hotel 139
Ferris Meadow Lake 92
Fortnum's Food Hall 189
Fudō Myō-ō statue 42

Garrick's Temple 92
Gay Hussar 61
Gerry's Wines and Spirits 135
Graff Diamonds 48
Ham House 91
Handel's house 198
Hyde Park, the wilder side 70
Italian Bookshop 144
Italian Gardens 144
Japan Centre 41
Japan, war declared on 74
Kensal Green Cemetery 150
Kensington Gardens, playing
   pirates in 120
Kew Palace 65
King Henry's Mound 66
King's Observatory 67
Kyoto Garden 40
Maison Bertaux 50
Millennium Maze 147
Milroy's of Soho 134
Naked Ladies 91
Nordic Bar 172
Norwegian boulder at Ranger's Lodge
   171
Notting Hill Carnival 114
100 Club 199
Original Maids of Honour Cake 65
Orleans House Gallery 91
Paddington station 150
Panorama Steel Band Competition 115
Piccadilly Art Market 19
Piccadilly Arts Festival 44
River Longford 66
St George's, Hanover Square 33
St James's Saturday market 44
Serpentine Lido 88
7 Hammersmith Terrace 26
ScandiKitchen 172
Speakers' Corner 160
Twickenham Museum 91
Wallace Collection 207
Wharncliffe Viaduct 147
Wheatsheaf 57
Wigmore Hall 198

INDEX

A

Aldwych tube station 199
Anglo-Saxon burial mounds 16
Apollo 10 201
Arsenal FC 132
art supplies 18
Arts and Crafts movement 18,
    24, 25, 26
Ashmole, Elias 44
Avenue, Sydenham 19

B

bats 70, 84, 110, 147
Bazalgette, Joseph 149, 150, 151
BBC Television 166
Beale, Edward 23
Bear Gardens 162
Beatles 197, 198, 199, 216
Berners-Lee, Tim 200
Berry Bros & Rudd 32
Betjeman, John 26, 36–8, 54,
    56, 145
birds 16
Blitz 72, 180
Bloomsbury Group 216
Bolívar, Simón, statue of 1 39
bookshops 144, 172, 184, 202,
    215–17
Boudicca, Queen 204
Bourgeois, Francis 19
Braithwaite, John 150
Brent Reservoir 148
Brick Lane 18
British Museum 30, 47, 94,
    144, 187
Brixton, Windrush Square
    named in 128

Brown's Hotel 75
Brunel, Isambard Kingdom
    147, 149, 150
Brunel, Marc Isambard 127, 150
Burgh House, Buttery Café 124
Burne-Jones, Edward 26, 27
butterflies 16

C

Cabinet War Rooms 74
cable car 156
Canaletto 143
Canary Wharf 156, 159
Capital Ring 69
caravanning 22
Carlton Gardens 50
Carow, Edith 33
Cater, John 23
Cavendish, Thomas 39
céilí dancing 129
cemeteries 70, 150, 163, 214
Chancery Lane Safe Deposit Co. 48
Charles II 22
Chartered Markets 182
Cheung family 14
Chinbrook Meadows,
    River Quaggy 111
Christmas carols 189
city farm 181
Columbus, Christopher,
    statue of 139
Conan Doyle, Arthur 175
Constable, John 17
Coombes Wood 13
Courtauld Gallery 51, 207
Courtauld, Samuel 51
Covent Garden, Tea House 95
cricket 132
Cross Bones 163
Crown Passage 186
Croydon, thousand years of 13
Crystal Palace Park,
    dinosaur hunting in 111
Crystal Palace transmitter 13

cycling:
Ingrebourne Valley and Hill 104
Lee Valley Velopark 82

D

Dando, John 26
Danish Church 172
Darwin, Charles 79, 111, 200
Davy, Humphry 200
dead-letter drops 59
Dell Bridge, bats on 70
Denmark Street 198
Deptford Creek, Peter the Great
    statue? 61
Diana Garden 66
Diana, Princess of Wales, Memorial
    Playground 120
Dickens, Charles 47, 173–5, 216
    Daughty Street home of 174
    Devonshire Terrace home of 175
Disraeli, Benjamin 33, 160
Docklands, Sailortown 119
Dollis Hill House 106
Dufour, Antoine 30
Dulwich Hamlet 131
Dulwich Picture Gallery 19
Dylan, Bob 199

E

Easter Island 30
Eliot, George 33
Emery Walker Trust 26
Empire Windrush, MV 128
Epping Forest 14
Execution Dock 119

F

Faraday, Michael 200, 202
Fitzrovia, Wheatsheaf 57
5a Bloomsbury Square,
    Pushkin House Trust 59
Fleming, Ian 122
Fox Hill 19
foxes 16

Franklin, Benjamin 31, 32
Franklin, Rosalind 200

G

Gladstone Park 106
Gladstone, William Ewart 160, 175
Go Ape 23
Graff jewellers 48
Great Eastern, SS 152
Great Western Railway 147, 150
Green Belt 12, 16, 76, 102
Greenwich Hospital Estate 22
Grimaldi, Joseph 212

H

Hackney Marshes:
blackberrying on 115
football on 84
Hainault Forest 103
Hampstead Lawn Billiards and
  Skittles Club 123
Hampstead Museum 124
Hampstead tube station 177
Hampton Court, Great Vine 67
Handel, George Frideric 127, 197
Hatton, Christopher 47
Hatton Garden 47
helicopter tour of London 154
Hewson, Polly 32
High Elms Estate 79
Highgate Cemetery 141, 214
History of Tea, V&A Museum 94
Hô Chí Minh 139
Holbein, Hans 17
Horse Guards Parade (Trooping
  of the Colour) 51, 87, 208
Hoxne 47
Hoxton Street 199
Hyde Park:
Serpentine Lido 88
Speakers' Corner 160
wilder side of 70

I

Imperial War Museum 22, 73
Institut Français du Royaume-Uni 52
Irish dancing 129
Iron Age pit 16
Isle of Dogs 119, 152, 179

J

Jack the Ripper 135
Jacob's Island 174
Japan–Britain Exhibition 39
Japan Festival (1992) 40
Jolly Roger flag 119
Joyden's Wood 78

K

Kapoor, Anish 154
Keats House 57
Keston Common 204
Kew, King's Observatory 67
Kew Gardens 65
Koh-i-Noor diamond 46

L

Landseer, Edwin 186
Lawes, Eric 47
L'Eglise Neuve, Brick Lane 51
Leicester Square, Frightfest 115
Lenin, Vladimir 140
Liberty Bell 34
Limehouse Basin 154
Lincoln, Abraham 32
Lincoln's Inn Fields (Soane's
  Museum) 159, 178
London Helicopter Centres 154
London Review of Books 217
London Review Cake Shop 216
London Rib Voyages 113
London Zoo 187
'Longplayer' 202
Lordship Lane 19
Louis Philippe II of France 91

M

martial-arts equipment 42
Marx, Karl 141, 160
Mayflower 31
Metropolitan Green Belt 12, 102
Mill Hill to Hampstead Health walk 71
Millennium Dome 156
MI6 building, Vauxhall 205
Moat Wood 23
Molly May (Thames boat) 92
Mond, Ludwig 30
Moo Canoes 154
Morris & Co. 25, 26
Morris, William 24, 25, 26, 160
Museum of Immigration and Diversity
  127
Museum of London Docklands 119

N

National Centre for Circus Arts 212
National Cycle Route 13
National Gallery 19, 30, 60, 143, 196
National Maritime Museum 96
National Portrait Gallery 160, 186
Neale, Thomas 47
Neolithic pottery 16
Neolithic stone axes 13
New Malden 127
Newe Ditch trackway 13
Newton, Isaac 200, 201
Nicholas II 47
Nicholson, John 44
Nicholson, Rosemary 44
nightingales 57
Northumberland Lodge 145

O

Oak Woods 23
Ognisko Restaurant 59
oldest art gallery 19
Olympic Games (2012) 81, 130, 132,
  154

Orpington, Crofton Royal Villa 78
Oddball, Max 213
Oxford vs Cambridge Goat Race 29

P

Palace of Westminster 159, 167
Pankhurst, Emmeline, statue of 140
Peter Pan stories 120
Pilgrim Fathers 31
Pissarro, Camille 19
pitch and putt 131
Polish Air Force 60
population and visitors 9
pubs 13, 29, 38, 106, 113, 119, 123,
   134, 135, 159, 164, 167, 171, 172,
   175, 179, 186, 187, 189, 201, 216

Q

Queen Elizabeth Hunting Park 154
Queen Elizabeth's Oak 22

R

RAF Hornchurch 75
RAF Northolt 60
Raphael 30
Richmond upon Thames municipal
   art gallery 91
Rolling Stones 198
Roman artefacts 16
Roman worship 205
Roupel Street, Kings Arms 113
Royal Botanic Gardens 65
Royal Festival Hall 56
Royal Garden Chinese Restaurant 14
Royal Greenwich Observatory 67
Royal Gunpowder Mills 84
Royal Parks 66, 70
Royal Yachting Association 77
Rubens, Peter Paul 17
rugby, home of 131

S

St George the Martyr 174
St Giles High Street 127

St James's Chapel 212
St James's Park, pelicans in 107
St Martin-in-the-Fields 178, 189
St Mary's Abbey, Stratford Langthorne
   81
St Nicholas's and St Luke's, Deptford
   119
St Pancras Hotel 199
St Paul's Cathedral 159
Sam Smith's 106
San Martín, José de, statue of 139
Savoy Steps 199
Sea Catch (Thames boat) 92
'secret burger' (Joe Allen) 33
Seven Dials 47
Shard 99, 159
Shelley, Percy 33
Shepperton, Ferris Meadow Lake 92
Sherlock Holmes stories 175, 216, 217
Sherwood Oak 16
Shooters Hill 14, 110
Shoreditch 18
Sir John Soane's Museum 159, 178
skittles, Freemasons Arms 123
Southwark Cathedral 205
Spitalfields 29, 51, 135
Stephenson's Rocket 201
Stevenson, Margaret 32
Stratford East, Theatre Royal 108
street art 18
Surrey Assize Rolls 16
Sustrans' Route 136 104
Swedenborg, Emanuel 172

T

Tangerine Dream Café, Chelsea Physic
   Garden 94
Tate Britain 20, 155, 161, 164
Tate Modern 69
tennis, history of 131
Thames:
speedboat on 113
swimming and boating on 92
Thames Barrier 156

Thames Ironworks and Shipbuilding
   Co. 108
3 Savile Row 199
Tower of London 46, 97–100, 192
Trees for Cities 23
Trinity Buoy 156
Trooping of the Colour (Horse Guards
   Parade) 51, 87, 208
Turner Prize 19
Turner, William 17, 155

U

Upminster Golf Course 103
Upper Lodge Water Fountain 66
US Embassy 33

V

V&A Museum 27, 47, 94, 122
Valence House Museum 194
Van Dyck, Anthony 17
vineyards 134

W

Warren's Blacking Factory 174
Watling Street 48
Webb, Philip 27
Wellington, Duke of 210
Wernher Collection 86
Westminster Abbey 54, 56
Westminster Village, pelicans in 107
Whipps Cross Lido 86
Whitehead, Joshua 29
Who 198
Wilderness, Greenwich Park 71
wildfowl 110
William Morris Society 26
Williams Wood 23
Windmill Hill, Fenton House 122
Windsor Castle 14
wine merchants 32, 134, 135
Wren, Christopher 201

Z

Zippos Circus 212

10 9 8 7 6 5 4

Virgin Books, an imprint of Ebury Publishing,
20 Vauxhall Bridge Road,
London SW1V 2SA

Virgin Books is part of the Penguin Random House group of companies
whose addresses can be found at global.penguinrandomhouse.com

Penguin
Random House
UK

Copyright © Tom Jones 2015

Tom Jones has asserted his right to be identified as the author of this
Work in accordance with the Copyright, Designs and Patents Act 1988

First published by Virgin Books in 2015

www.eburypublishing.co.uk

A CIP catalogue record for this book is available from the British Library

ISBN 9780753556269

Illustrations by David Doran
Design by Maru Studio

Printed and bound in India by Replika Press Pvt. Ltd.

MIX
Paper from
responsible sources
FSC   FSC® C018179
www.fsc.org

Penguin Random House is committed to a sustainable
future for our business, our readers and our planet.
This book is made from Forest Stewardship
Council® certified paper.